T0220595

Pro iOS Security and Forensics

Enterprise iPhone and iPad Safety

Eric Butow

Apress®

Pro iOS Security and Forensics

Eric Butow
Jackson, California, USA

ISBN-13 (pbk): 978-1-4842-3756-4   ISBN-13 (electronic): 978-1-4842-3757-1
https://doi.org/10.1007/978-1-4842-3757-1

Library of Congress Control Number: 2018952358

Managing Director, Apress Media LLC: Welmoed Spahr
Acquisitions Editor: Aaron Black
Development Editor: James Markham
Coordinating Editor: Jessica Vakili

Cover designed by eStudioCalamar

Cover image designed by Freepik (www.freepik.com)

Distributed to the book trade worldwide by Springer Science+Business Media New York, 233 Spring Street, 6th Floor, New York, NY 10013. Phone 1-800-SPRINGER, fax (201) 348-4505, e-mail orders-ny@springer-sbm.com, or visit www.springeronline.com. Apress Media, LLC is a California LLC and the sole member (owner) is Springer Science + Business Media Finance Inc (SSBM Finance Inc). SSBM Finance Inc is a **Delaware** corporation.

For information on translations, please e-mail rights@apress.com, or visit http://www.apress.com/rights-permissions.

Apress titles may be purchased in bulk for academic, corporate, or promotional use. eBook versions and licenses are also available for most titles. For more information, reference our Print and eBook Bulk Sales web page at http://www.apress.com/bulk-sales.

Any source code or other supplementary material referenced by the author in this book is available to readers on GitHub via the book's product page, located at www.apress.com/978-1-4842-3756-4. For more detailed information, please visit http://www.apress.com/source-code.

Printed on acid-free paper

For my grandmother,
Clara Butow (1912-2008), whose lessons,
spoken and unspoken, continue to teach me

Table of Contents

About the Author

Eric Butow is the owner and CEO of Butow Communications Group (BCG) in Jackson, California, which offers online marketing ROI improvement services for businesses. He has used iPhones in his business since he bought the 3G in 2008. Eric has authored or co-authored 31 books, most recently *My Samsung Galaxy S7, Samsung Gear S2 for Dummies*, and *Instagram for Business for Dummies*. He has also developed and taught networking, computing, and usability courses for Ed2Go, Virtual Training Company, California State University, Sacramento, and Udemy.

Acknowledgments

My thanks to the best literary agent on the planet, Carole Jelen. I also thank and appreciate my editors, Jessica Vakili and Aaron Black, for all their help and support. And I thank you for buying and reading this book.

CHAPTER 1

Preparing Security Features

With iOS security features as with most of Apple's efforts, the company strives to make it easy for its customers to use its products. In the case of managing a large number of its devices in a corporate setting, Apple makes the Device Enrollment Program (DEP) available on its website for network administrators to set up iPhones (as well as iPads and Macs) without having to configure each physical device.

After you sign up with DEP, you'll talk with an Apple business representative on the phone, as you'll learn about later in this chapter. During the call, you'll learn whether you're ready to go or if you need to make some changes to qualify for DEP.

What iPhones Are Eligible?

Before you start enrolling in DEP, you need to take stock of the iPhones you're going to administer in your organization.

If your business purchased iPhones through its Apple business account for business use only, and those devices were purchased after March 1, 2011, then you're ready to enroll.

© Eric Butow 2018
E. Butow, *Pro iOS Security and Forensics*, https://doi.org/10.1007/978-1-4842 3757-1_1

Your business may have a Bring Your Own Device (BYOD) policy for some or all its employees. If so, you can enroll each user's personal iPhone in DEP to manage. Apple determines if an iPhone is eligible for DEP by the location where that iPhone was purchased. For example, if the iPhone was purchased through a cellular carrier such as Verizon or AT&T, then Apple may accept that iPhone into DEP.

An iPhone purchased directly from Apple using a consumer account is not eligible. Your employee may be able to get their phone number moved from a consumer to a business account so the phone can be added to DEP. They will have to contact their cellular carrier to find out if they are eligible and to go through the transfer process, which may take some time.

Note   Check your employees' phones to ensure they have the latest version of iOS 11 installed so they have access to the latest security and management features. If your company requires all the features iOS 11 offers and one or more employees have older iPhones that can't run iOS 11, you will need to speak with those employees and/or management to determine if those employees need to purchase a new iPhone or be supplied with an iPhone assigned by your business.

Enroll Your Devices

Access the Device Enrollment Program website at `https://www.apple.com/business/dep/`. Scroll down the page to view more information about the program. Enrollment is a multi-part process, so get comfortable and have your favorite beverage nearby before you start.

Create Your New Apple ID

The first step in the process is to create a new Apple ID. As part of the application, you will have to enter a new email address for DEP that is different from any other email address you use.

1. Click or tap Enroll Now shown in Figure 1-1.

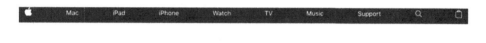

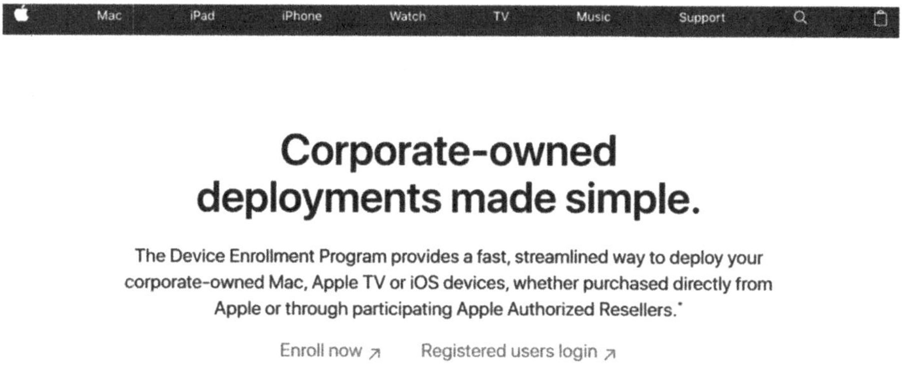

Mac
iPad
iPhone
Watch
TV
Music
Support
Corporate-owned deployments made simple.
The Device Enrollment Program provides a fast, streamlined way to deploy your corporate-owned Mac, Apple TV or iOS devices, whether purchased directly from Apple or through participating Apple Authorized Resellers.*
Enroll now ↗
Registered users login ↗

Figure 1-1. *The Enroll Now link appears near the top of the page*

2. In the Welcome webpage, click or tap Enroll to the right of the Device Enrollment Program description. See Figure 1-2.

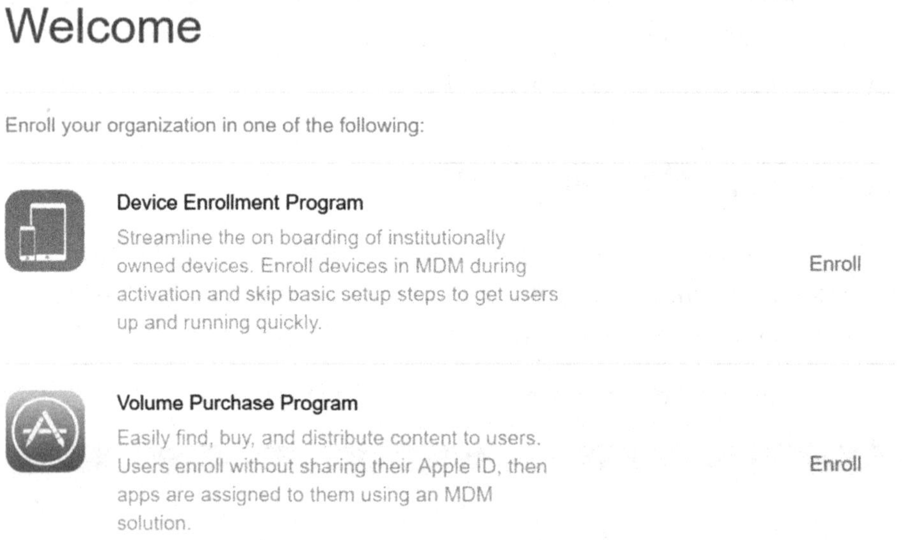

Welcome

Enroll your organization in one of the following:

Device Enrollment Program

Streamline the on boarding of institutionally owned devices. Enroll devices in MDM during activation and skip basic setup steps to get users up and running quickly.

Enroll

Volume Purchase Program

Easily find, buy, and distribute content to users. Users enroll without sharing their Apple ID, then apps are assigned to them using an MDM solution.

Enroll

Figure 1-2. *The Device Enrollment Program entry appears at the top of the webpage*

4

3. In the Your Details webpage, type your company details into the appropriate boxes and then click Next as shown in Figure 1-3.

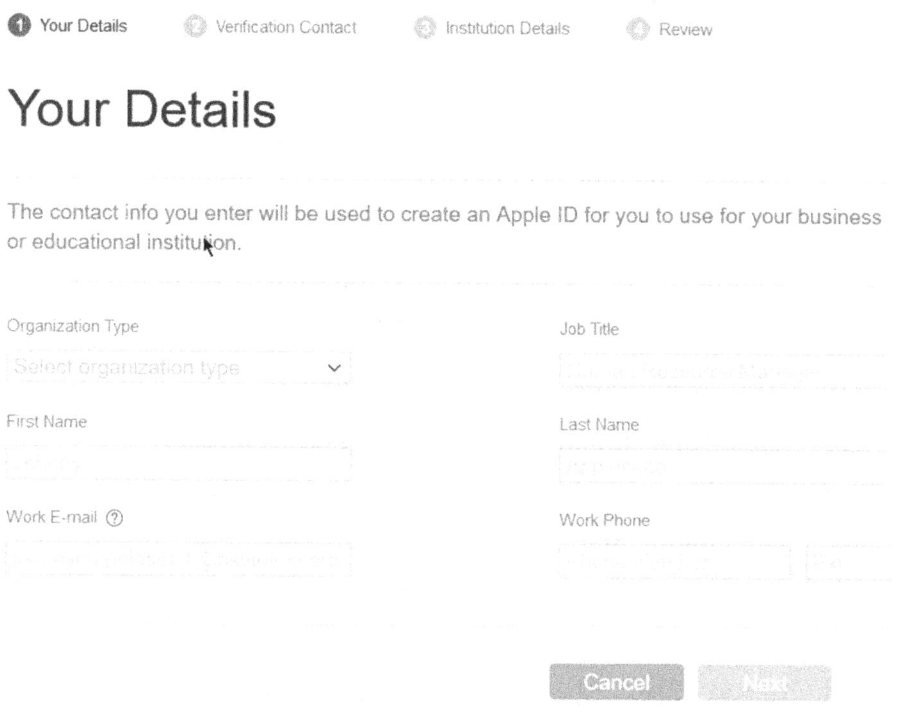

Your Details

The contact info you enter will be used to create an Apple ID for you to use for your business or educational institution.

Figure 1-3. *The Your Details webpage is the first of four steps in the application*

4. When you receive an email message from Apple that contains the next steps to enroll in DEP, click the Sign In button within the email message.

5. In the new browser tab, type the user name and temporary password that appears in the email message and then press Enter (or tap Return) on your keyboard.

5

6. Update your Apple ID with your new password and then click or tap Change Password.

7. Click or tap Continue to verify your email address. In a short while, a message from Apple appears in your email inbox. This message contains a six-digit code.

8. Return to your browser, type the code into the browser, and then click or tap Continue.

9. Now enter your complete birthdate and the three security questions (and answers) you want to use in case you can't remember your password.

10. When you're done, click or tap Update.

11. Once Apple updates your ID, click or tap Continue.

12. Now type your name and password and then press Enter (or tap Return).

13. Answer two of the three security questions you added earlier and then click or tap Continue.

14. Within the Security section in the Apple ID webpage, click Get Started under Two-Step Verification. See Figure 1-4.

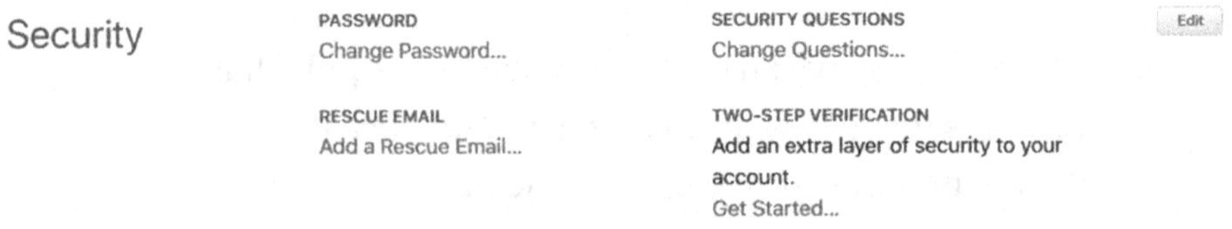

| Security | PASSWORD
Change Password... | SECURITY QUESTIONS
Change Questions... | Edit |
| | RESCUE EMAIL
Add a Rescue Email... | TWO-STEP VERIFICATION
Add an extra layer of security to your account.
Get Started... | |

Figure 1-4. *The Get Started link appears in the lower-right of the Security section*

15. When you finish reading about two-step verification in the window, click Continue.

16. Type the phone number you want to use to receive verification codes when you sign in with your Apple ID, and then click or tap Continue.

17. Type the four-digit code you received in the text message on your phone and then click or tap Continue.

18. If you have another Apple mobile device that has Find My iPhone, iPad, or iPod touch enabled, you will have to verify your devices in the same way you did in the previous step. When you finish verifying those devices, or you don't see any devices to verify, click or tap Continue.

19. Print or write down your recovery key in case you can't remember your password or you lose the iPhone you're using to set up your DEP account.

20. When you're done, click or tap Continue.

21. Type your Recovery Key and then click or tap Confirm.

22. Review the Two-Step Verification conditions and then click or tap the I Understand the Conditions Above check box.

23. Click or tap Enable Two-Step Verification.

24. Click or tap Done.

In a few minutes, you'll receive a verification message from Apple in your email app.

Add Your Business Details

Once you've created your new Apple ID, click or switch to the Apple Deployment Programs tab in your browser. Click or tap Deploy.apple.com as you see in Figure 1-5.

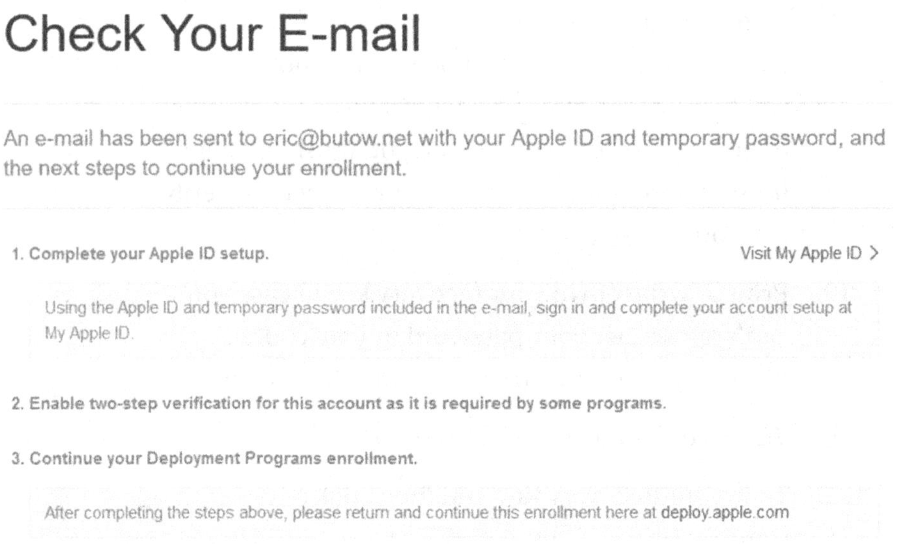

Check Your E-mail

An e-mail has been sent to eric@butow.net with your Apple ID and temporary password, and the next steps to continue your enrollment.

---

1. Complete your Apple ID setup.   Visit My Apple ID >

   Using the Apple ID and temporary password included in the e-mail, sign in and complete your account setup at My Apple ID.

2. Enable two-step verification for this account as it is required by some programs.

3. Continue your Deployment Programs enrollment.

   After completing the steps above, please return and continue this enrollment here at deploy.apple.com

Figure 1-5. *The link to deploy and continue appears below step 3 on the webpage*

Now you need to add your business details to your DEP application as follows:

1. In the Deployment Programs webpage, type your Apple ID and password, and then click or tap Sign In.

2. Verify your identity using two-step verification by clicking or tapping the phone number you want to use (if necessary), and then click or tap Continue.

3. Type the four-digit verification code you received in the text message on your iPhone and then click or tap Continue.

4. In the Add Verification Contact Details webpage, enter the contact information for the person who can verify that you have the legal authority to sign up for DEP.

Note   If you signed up for DEP and can also supply legal authority, you need to type a different email address in Step 4 than the one you used to sign up for DEP.

---

5. When you're done, click or tap Next.

6. In the Add Institution Details webpage shown in Figure 1-6, type your institution information and the DUNS number.

7. When you're finished, tap Next.

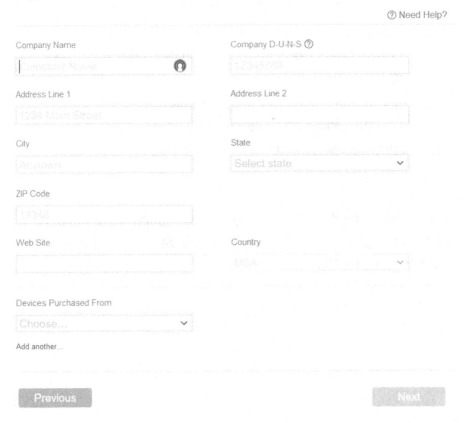

Figure 1-6. *Begin adding your institutional details by typing your company name in the Company Name box*

Tip You can find your DUNS number by clicking the blue help icon to the right of Company D-U-N-S and then clicking or tapping "Locate your company's D-U-N-S Number" in the window. The Dun & Bradstreet website opens in a new browser tab opens so you can read all the information the website requires to obtain your DUNS number.

8. When you receive your DUNS number, copy the number from the Dun & Bradstreet website page, return to the Deployment Programs tab in your browser, and then paste the number in the Company D-U-N-S box.

9. Return to the Dun & Bradstreet tab, log out, and then return to the Deployment Programs tab.

10. After you enter the reseller ID number, click or tap Verify under the number to verify that the number is correct.

11. Type your address, city, ZIP code, and website address in the appropriate boxes.

12. Select your state and country from the State and Country drop-down boxes, respectively.

13. Click the Devices Purchased From check box and then select whether you purchased your phones from a reseller (such as Verizon or AT&T) or from Apple Direct.

14. Enter your Apple customer ID or DEP Reseller ID number.

Note   If you don't have your DEP Reseller ID number, you can search for this information on your reseller website.

---

15. When you're finished, click or tap Next.

16. After you finish reviewing your enrollment details, click or tap Submit.

17. Now you need to verify your identity with two-step notification, so select the phone number you want to use to verify your identity (if necessary) and then click or tap Continue.

18. Type the verification code you received in the messaging app of the device you used, and then click or tap Continue.

Wait Your Turn

Now the Deployment Programs webpage shows you that your Device Enrollment Program application is in review. It may take Apple up to five business days to review your application. When the review is complete, you'll receive a phone call from Apple at the number you entered in the Your Details webpage.

A helpful Apple representative will ask you a few follow-up questions to ensure that you are who you say you are and that you can meet all of Apple's requirements. Once you answer the questions to Apple's satisfaction, the representative will tell you that you're approved, and a day or two later you'll receive an email message (see Figure 1-7) telling you what to do now that you're approved.

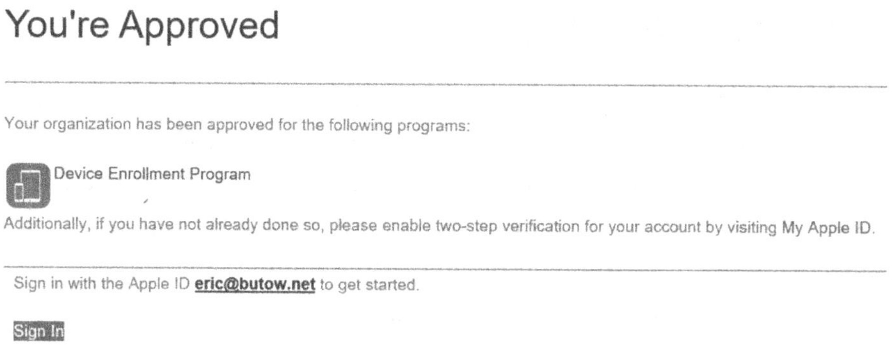

You're Approved

Your organization has been approved for the following programs:

 Device Enrollment Program

Additionally, if you have not already done so, please enable two-step verification for your account by visiting My Apple ID.

Sign in with the Apple ID **eric@butow.net** to get started.

Sign In

Figure 1-7. *A sample DEP approval e-mail from Apple*

The Final Steps

Once you're approved, begin the setup process by clicking or tapping Sign In within the email message. In the Deployment Programs webpage in your browser, type your username and password into the appropriate boxes and then click or tap Sign In.

In the Verify Your Identity webpage, select the phone number where you want to receive your access code and then click or tap Continue. (If you only have one phone number, it's selected automatically.)

After you type the new code in the Enter Verification Code window, click or tap Continue. Now go through the last four setup steps: The fun tasks of agreeing to the terms and conditions for the DEP, macOS, iOS, and tvOS Software License Agreements. It's up to you if you want to read any of the Terms and Conditions on each page.

In every page, you need to click or tap the check box to the left of the "I have read and agree to..." sentence below the terms and conditions, and then click or tap Agree.

Now You Can Start

Once you've agreed to all the terms and conditions, the Welcome webpage appears (see Figure 1-8). On the left side of the webpage, you can click links to show a list of company administrators, view more information about DEP, and refresh your memory about the terms and conditions. Return to the Welcome webpage by clicking or tapping Deployment Programs in the upper-left corner of the page.

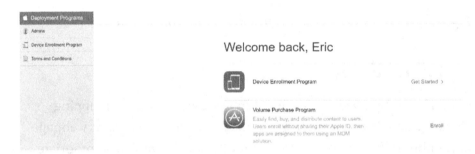

Figure 1-8. *The Get Started link appears to the right of the Device Enrollment Program logo*

In the upper-right corner of the webpage shown in Figure 1-9, click your name to view a drop-down menu to get your organizational details, send feedback to Apple, or sign out. You can also click or tap the Help icon to open the help documentation window.

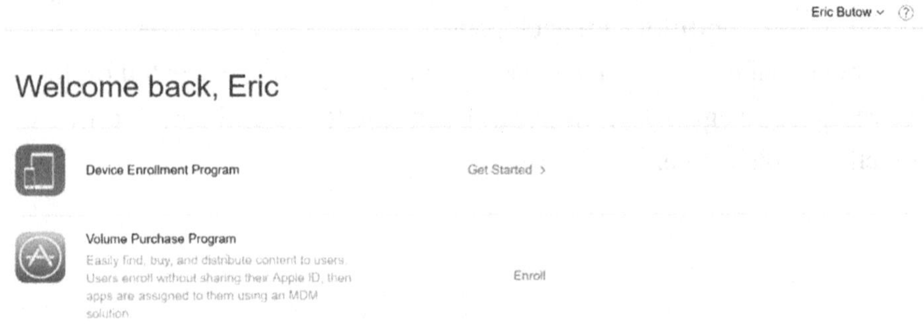

Figure 1-9. *The Help icon is a question mark inside a circle*

When you're ready to start, click or tap Get Started.

Note   If the webpage is idle for about 10 minutes, you're logged out automatically; if you want to get back in, you'll need to re-enter your username, password, and verification code.

Find Your MDM

One of the issues that the Apple representative will remind you about in your phone conversation is the need to acquire and set up a Mobile Device Management (MDM) server on your Windows PC or Mac, or from an MDM provider's server if you decide to use a cloud-based solution.

An MDM server is an app you need to perform a wide variety of tasks to manage your company iPhones, including, but not limited to these:

- Securing email messages

- Securing corporate documents

- Remote device locking

- Creating predefined Wi-Fi settings for your office

- Enforcing any other computing policies such as Internet use

It's easy to find a list of MDM providers online. Each solution provides a list of features so you can ensure that it meets your company's needs. After you select an MDM provider, you need to add the MDM server to the DEP so you can configure your iPhone management settings.

For this book, I'll use SimpleMDM, which is a cloud-based MDM app you can use from any computer or tablet, and it has a good combination of features at a low price. It even has a 30-day free trial (see Figure 1-10) after you sign up. You can access the website and view more information at `https://simplemdm.com/`.

 SimpleMDM   Features   Pricing   Sign In   **Try For Free**

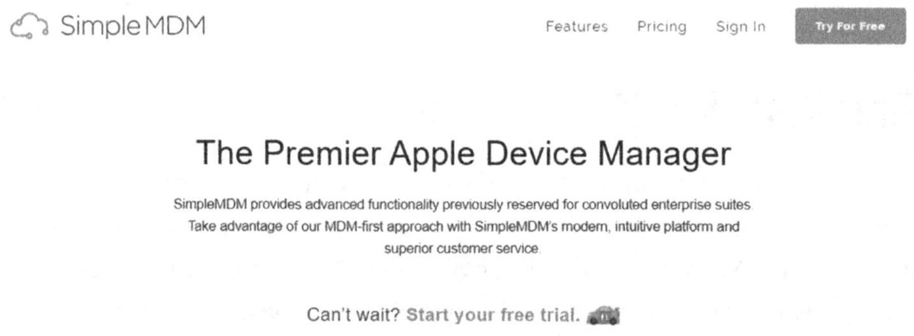

The Premier Apple Device Manager

SimpleMDM provides advanced functionality previously reserved for convoluted enterprise suites.
Take advantage of our MDM-first approach with SimpleMDM's modern, intuitive platform and
superior customer service.

Can't wait? Start your free trial.

Figure 1-10. *Scroll up and down the SimpleMDM home page to learn more about the app*

Download, install, and set up your MDM server before you proceed to the next section.

Note   If you decide SimpleMDM is not the right solution for your business, just type **mobile device management** into your favorite search engine to see other MDM app websites and reviews.

Add Your MDM to DEP

Switch or open a new browser tab and open the DEP webpage and then click or tap Get Started in the Welcome page. The Manage Servers webpage appears (see Figure 1-11) so you can add your MDM server.

Manage Servers   Add MDM Server

No MDM Servers

Figure 1-11. *There are no MDM servers listed when you open the Manage Servers screen for the first time*

In the upper-left area of the webpage, you see an expanded menu that includes options to manage your servers and devices, and to view your assignment history, such as when you assigned an iPhone to your list of devices to manage.

Note   Once you have set up your MDM server, the server may allow you to add the MDM from its website. Since every MDM is different, this example uses the Apple DEP website to add your MDM.

Click or tap Add MDM Server to open the Add MDM Server window and begin the three-step addition process.

Step 1: Enter Your MDM Server Name

Type your MDM server name as shown in Figure 1-12, and then click or tap Next.

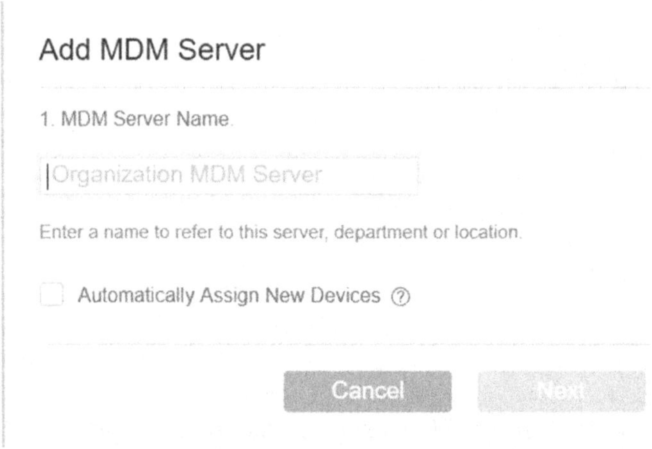

Add MDM Server

1. MDM Server Name.

| |Organization MDM Server |

Enter a name to refer to this server, department or location.

☐ Automatically Assign New Devices ⑦

Cancel   Next

Figure 1-12. *Step one of the three-step MDM server addition process*

Now you need to download your DEP Public Key from your MDM app. To do this, click Settings in the menu on the left side of the webpage (see Figure 1-13) and then click or tap DEP.

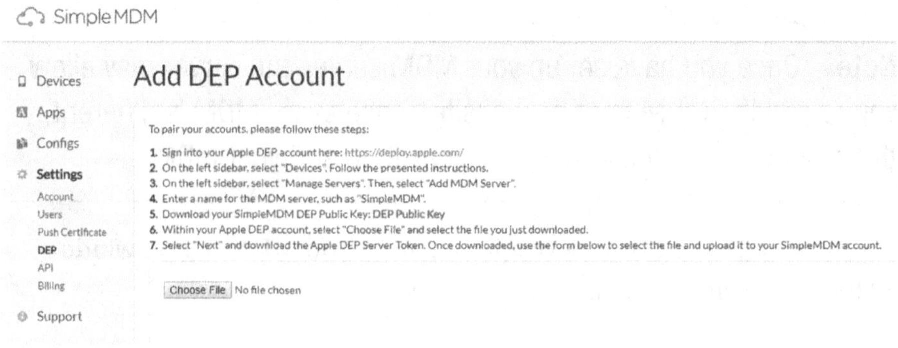

Figure 1-13. *You only need to pay attention to step 5 in the Add DEP Account instructions*

In the Add DEP Account webpage, click DEP Public Key, which you see in step 5 within the list of instructions. SimpleMDM downloads the key file to your browser's default downloads folder.

Step 2: Add the Key

Return to the DEP webpage tab and add the public key within the Add window as follows:

1. Click or tap Choose File.

2. Navigate to the downloads folder if necessary and open the file.

3. Click or tap Next.

Step 3: Get Your Token

After you add the key, click or tap Your Server Token to download from Apple the server token that you can install on your MDM server. The token file downloads to your browser's default downloads folder. When you're finished, click or tap Done.

What's Next?

The Manage Servers webpage list now shows your server name, the number of devices connected (0), and when the devices were last connected (Never). Now you need to add the server token to your MDM.

In the Add DEP Account webpage within SimpleMDM, click or tap Choose File, open the server token file, and then click or tap Upload. Now you see your DEP account information, which you can update. When you're done, click or tap Save. Now you see your DEP account within the list in the DEP Accounts webpage.

After you return to the DEP website and view the list in the Manage Servers webpage, the server list shows that you were last connected to the MDM today and shows the last connected Internet Protocol (IP) address.

View and change the server information (such as the server name) by clicking on the server name in the list within the Server Details window. Close the window by clicking or tapping OK.

Enroll a Device to Your MDM

Before you add a device to DEP, you need to add the device to your MDM server. In SimpleMDM, the Devices webpage shows no devices, but you can add your iPhone by clicking or tapping the "enroll your first device" link (see Figure 1-14).

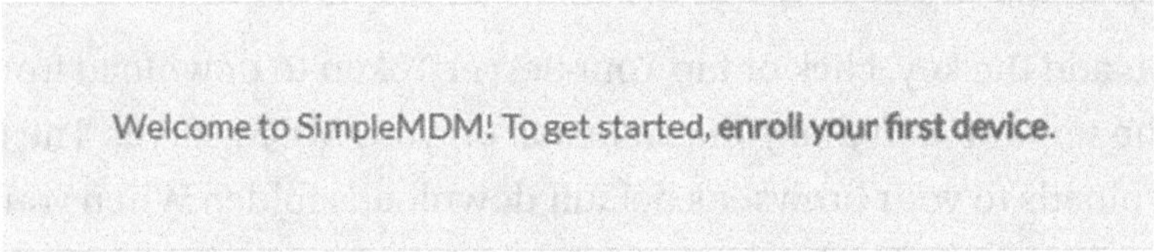

Welcome to SimpleMDM! To get started, **enroll your first device.**

Figure 1-14. *The link appears in the center of the screen*

Now follow these steps to enroll your device:

1. In the Enroll a Device webpage, click or tap Create Enrollment.

2. If there is a specific device group you want to use, click or tap Default and then select the group from the list.

3. Type your preferred iPhone name into the Device Name box.

4. Click or tap Create.

5. In the Enroll Device webpage, open your iPhone Camera app and point your camera at the QR code (see Figure 1-15), or type the phone number or email address to which you want to send the enrollment data into the Send to Device box.

6. When you're done, click or tap Send.

Figure 1-15. *You can't miss the QR code on the left side of the screen*

For this example, I pointed my iPhone camera at the QR code. A message on your iPhone asks you to open the Safari browser. Once you're in the browser, a message window pops up and asks you to open the Settings screen. Tap Allow in the window to display the Install Profile screen shown in Figure 1-16.

Figure 1-16. *Tap More Details to learn more about the profile you'll be installing*

7. Tap Install in the Install Profile screen.

8. Type your iPhone passcode.

9. After you read the warning in the Warning screen, tap Install.

10. Tap Trust in the Remote Management window.

11. After the iPhone installs the profile, tap Done.

12. After a few seconds, the App Installation window appears; tap Install to install the SimpleMDM app.

Note   If you can't install SimpleMDM, you'll see the Verification Required window, which requires you to verify your App Store payment information. Tap Continue to update your account in the Account Settings screen. When you're done, the iPhone will install SimpleMDM.

13. In the App Store window in the bottom of the screen, tap Install.

14. After you finish installing the app, press the Home button to see the Simple MDM icon on your iPhone Home screen.

15. Open SimpleMDM by tapping the SimpleMDM icon.

16. Your first decision is to determine whether you want SimpleMDM to send you notifications; tap Allow in the window.

17. A message window asks if the app can access your location or not; tap Always Allow.

You're all done. The screen says location tracking is enabled. When you return to the SimpleMDM website, click or tap Devices and you see that your iPhone has been added to the device list.

Sync with Apple DEP

With SimpleMDM set up on your iPhone, now you need to sync with Apple DEP. Here's how to do that from within SimpleMDM:

1. In the menu on the left side of the SimpleMDM webpage, click or tap Settings.

2. Under the Settings menu header, click or tap DEP.

3. In the DEP Accounts webpage, click or tap Sync with Apple on the right side of the screen.

After a few seconds, a message pops up at the top of the screen that says your MDM is synced with DEP and you're ready to manage your iPhone(s).

Setting Up Apps

After you install your device in SimpleMDM, you can view a list of apps currently installed on your iPhone, request management of those apps by SimpleMDM, and update or delete the SimpleMDM app itself.

SimpleMDM allows you to add a wide variety of apps, including these:

- Public App Store apps

- Private B2B VPP apps

- IPA binary files

If you're not in the Devices webpage, click or tap Devices in the menu on the left side of the page. In the Devices webpage, click or tap the device name in the list. Within the Device Details page, click or tap Apps. A list of apps that you currently have installed appears in the Apps list (see Figure 1-17).

Figure 1-17. *The list of apps appears in alphabetical order*

At the right side of each app entry, manage the app by clicking or tapping the Request Management button within the Actions column. You see the Request Management button change to two buttons: Update (to update the app to the current version) and Delete (to delete the app altogether).

When you update an app, you'll see an App Update alert on your iPhone Home screen telling you that an update is pending. Press the Home button to unlock your iPhone and then update the app by tapping Update in the window.

For this example, request management of the Gmail app. On the iPhone, an alert message in the Lock screen tells you about a request to change your app management. After you press the Home button, tap Manage in the App Management Change window.

Within the Device Details webpage in SimpleMDM, the Request Management button changes to Management Requested.

Deploy Your App Catalog

Before you can deploy apps to your iPhone(s), you need to select apps
and then add them to your catalog. Next, you need to add the apps to app
groups that will deploy to all your iPhones. Finally, you'll learn how to
push assigned apps to all your iPhones or one specific iPhone.

Add an App

You add apps by clicking or tapping Apps within the menu on the left-side
of the screen. Now, within the App Catalog webpage, do the following:

1. Click or tap Add App on the right side of the screen.

2. In the drop-down list, click or tap Apple Store App
    as you see in Figure 1-18.

Figure 1-18. *The Apple Store App is the location for all iPhone apps*

3. In the Add Apple Store App webpage, type the
    search term(s) for the app you want in the Search
    Terms box.

Tip   If you want to search for apps in a country Apple Store that's outside the United States, click United States and then click or tap the country name in the drop-down list. When you're done, click Search.

4. The list of iOS apps appears on the webpage with Gmail at the top of the list as shown in Figure 1-19. Within the Gmail row, click or tap Add.

Figure 1-19. *The Add button appears at the right of the Gmail row in the list*

The App Catalog webpage appears and you see Gmail in the app list. The next step is to deploy the app to all the iPhones you manage.

Add App Groups and Deploy

Start the deployment process by placing the app, which is Gmail in this example, into an app group, and then install one or more apps in the group to your iPhones. Here's how to do it:

1. Under Apps in the menu on the left side of the screen, click or tap Assignment.

27

2. In the App Assignment webpage, click or tap Add
    App Group (see Figure 1-20).

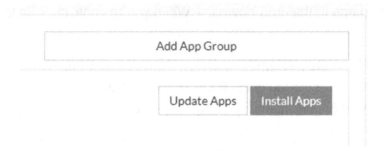

Figure 1-20. *The Add App Group button appears in the upper-right*
area of the App Assignment window

3. In the New App Group webpage, type the name of
    your app group in the Name box.

4. Click or tap Save. The name of your group appears at
    the top of the list, and three drop-down lists appear
    within your group:

    a. Click or tap Add App, and then click or tap the
        name of the app you want to add within the
        drop-down list.

    b. If you're going to add an app to a group of
        iPhones, click or tap Add Device Group and
        then click or tap Default in the drop-down list.

    c. If you're going to add an app to just one iPhone,
        click or tap Add Device and then click or tap the
        device name in the drop-down list.

5. Click or tap the Install Apps button, which appears
    just below the Add App Group button.

On your iPhone Lock screen, you see an alert informing you that SimpleMDM is about to install the app from the App Store and manage the app on your phone.

Install the app by pressing the Home button and then tapping Install within the App Installation window. After SimpleMDM installs the app, you can tap the app icon on the iPhone screen and use the app.

Push Assigned Apps

If you have one iPhone that's missing a required app that the rest of your iPhones have (and that your company requires), you can push an assigned app to that affected iPhone. Here's how:

1. Click or tap Devices in the menu on the left side of the SimpleMDM webpage.

2. In the Devices webpage, click or tap the name of the iPhone.

3. In the upper-right corner of the Device Details webpage, click or tap Actions.

4. Click or tap Push Assigned Apps in the drop-down list.

The notice that Assigned apps have been pushed to the device appears at the top of the webpage for a few seconds. Then watch your iPhone for an alert on your Lock screen that SimpleMDM is going to install the affected app(s) on your phone, and you can install the apps as you learned to do earlier in this chapter.

Manage Your Configurations

If you need to manage your configurations to limit what your users can and cannot use in an app on their iPhone, here's how to do it:

1. Under Apps in the menu on the left side of the screen, click or tap Catalog.

2. In the App Catalog webpage, click or tap the app name in the list.

3. In the App webpage, click or tap Manage Configuration.

4. Now click or tap the green Add icon shown in Figure 1-21.

Figure 1-21. *The Add icon appears below the Key column in the list*

You've just added a new configuration entry row on the webpage. Now you need to add your configuration:

1. Type the key in the Key box.

2. Click or tap on the Value Type box and then click or tap the value type in the drop-down list.

3. Type the value in the value box.

You may need to consult the app documentation for information about how to enter correct configuration information. For example, if you want to manage your Gmail configuration, go to the Google website at `https://support.google.com/work/android/answer/7065453?hl=en` for instructions.

If you want to add more configurations, repeat the three steps just shown. When you're finished adding configurations, click or tap Save.

SimpleMDM automatically pushes the new configuration to the app on your iPhone(s). For example, if you add a default signature configuration, that signature will appear at the bottom of all sent email messages automatically.

CHAPTER 2

Using Security Apps and Backup

MDM systems contain a variety of security options to make sure that your iPhone users' data stay safe. SimpleMDM is no exception. These options include the ability to lock the screen, and, if your employee's iPhone is lost or stolen, you can take actions to remove the iPhone's passcode as well as wipe its data.

You can add security apps to your managed iPhones in SimpleMDM as you can with any other app. For example, you can download apps that block malicious websites. However, there are no anti-malware apps for iPhones as there are for computers, because Apple designed the iPhone in such a way that hackers cannot do the kinds of things needed to infect an iPhone.

As part of your company's security strategy, your employees may already be backing up their iPhones' data on iCloud or another file storage service such as Google Drive. Employees may also be using iTunes on their Windows PC or Mac to back up their iPhones' data to their computers.

In these cases, you need to create a set backup policy for all employee iPhones to ensure that all data is being backed up securely and regularly. Later in this chapter, you'll learn how to back up iPhones using the security features of iCloud and iTunes.

© Eric Butow 2018
E. Butow, *Pro iOS Security and Forensics*, https://doi.org/10.1007/978-1-4842-3757-1_2

However, these security measures may not be enough, and you may need to have much more control over your employees' iPhones. Many MDM providers, including SimpleMDM, allow close supervision of one or a group of iPhones to limit how data is shared and the apps employees can use.

Note   If your iPhones are supervised, it's highly recommended that you use supervision with company-provided iPhones. The Supervised iPhones option resets the content and settings of a device, which may be unacceptable to employees who want to use their own iPhones for both work and personal use. You'll learn more about decisions you have to make regarding company and personal iPhones in Chapter 4.

Taking Specific Security Actions

If you believe there is an issue that requires you to inform one of your company's iPhone users about it, SimpleMDM makes it easy for you to send a message to an individual iPhone to communicate information and/ or ask that employee to contact you.

If you realize that you have an urgent security problem, such as the loss or theft of an employee's iPhone, then you can lock the iPhone's screen, remove its passcode, and wipe its data in SimpleMDM.

The security options appear in a drop-down menu within the device information webpage. Here's how to open the menu:

1. If you're not in the Devices webpage already, click or tap Devices in the menu on the left side of the webpage.

2. Click or tap the name of the iPhone in the Devices list.

3. Click or tap the Actions button in the upper-right
    corner of the Device Details webpage (see Figure 2-1).

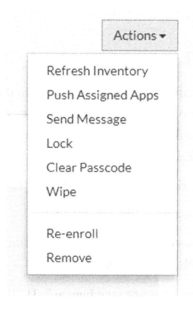

Figure 2-1. *The Actions drop-down menu appears underneath the*
button

Send a Message

Send a message to the iPhone user by clicking or tapping Send Message in
the drop-down menu. The Message Device webpage shown in Figure 2-2
allows you to type your message within the Message box.

Figure 2-2. *Make sure your message contains only the information*
you need to convey

When you finish typing the message, click or tap Message Device.
The Device Details webpage reappears, and your message appears on the
iPhone's Lock screen a few seconds after you send it.

Lock the Screen

If you suspect that an employee's iPhone is lost or in the possession of
someone who's not authorized to use it, you can lock the iPhone and
include a message that asks the person to call you to return it—perhaps in
exchange for a reward. Here's how:

1. In the Actions drop-down menu, click or tap Lock.

2. Type your message in the Message box.

3. Type the phone number you want the iPhone user
    to call in the Phone Number box.

4. Click or tap Lock Device (see Figure 2-3).

Figure 2-3. *The blue Lock Device button appears below and to the
right of the Phone Number box*

The Device Details webpage appears within SimpleMDM. On the
iPhone, the locked iPhone displays the title "Lost iPhone" along with your
message (if any), and asks you to call the number on the screen by tapping
the green Call button.

Once you have retrieved the iPhone and verified that it's in good
physical condition, press the Home button and then log in by tapping the
four-digit passcode. Now tap Settings in Apple ID Verification to open the
Settings screen and sign in using the employee's Apple password.

Tip   Before you return the iPhone to the employee, you may want to check to see that's it's operating properly. For example, verify that the iPhone can connect to the company network.

Clear the Passcode

If one of your iPhone users can't gain access to their iPhone using their password, clear the passcode in SimpleMDM by clicking or tapping Clear Passcode in the Actions drop-down menu.

In the pop-up window that appears at the top of the screen, remove the passcode by clicking or tapping OK. The next time you turn the iPhone on and then tap the Home button, the Home screen appears so you can start using the iPhone.

When you give the iPhone back to the employee, ensure that he adds a new passcode. If he's not sure how, give him these instructions:

1. Tap Settings in the Home screen.

2. In the Settings screen, tap Touch ID & Passcode.

3. In the Touch ID & Passcode screen, tap Turn Passcode On.

4. In the Set Passcode screen, tap Passcode Options above the keypad to choose to create a custom alphanumeric code, a custom numeric code, or a four-digit numeric code. The default option is a six-digit numeric code.

5. Type the passcode.

6. Verify the passcode by typing it again.

7. Type your Apple ID password to adopt the new passcode and complete the process.

As soon as you see that the user has reached the Set Passcode screen, you may want to ask if you should look away discreetly while he enters his passcode and Apple ID password to respect his privacy.

Caution   Clearing your passcode also removes your fingerprint(s) from the Touch ID feature on your iPhone, so your employee will have to add your fingerprint(s) again after you set your new password. What's more, if you have any services on the iPhone that require a passcode to use, such as Apple Pay, then those services will be deactivated and the employee will have to set them up again, too.

Wipe Data

If you learn that an employee's iPhone has been lost or stolen and there's no chance of retrieving it, it's important to wipe the data off that iPhone as soon as possible to block any opportunity for anyone to access sensitive company data. If the data is backed up, as described later in this chapter, then you'll be able to restore the data once the employee retrieves the iPhone or receives a new one.

Wipe an iPhone's data within SimpleMDM by clicking or tapping Wipe in the Actions drop-down menu. In the Wipe Device screen, type the serial number of the iPhone in the Serial Number box. The serial number is in bold type in the sentence above the box.

After you type the serial number, click or tap the red Wipe Device button. Once SimpleMDM sends the Wipe Device command, the iPhone turns off. It's likely the person who stole or discovers the iPhone will turn it on, but he will be disappointed to find that doing so completes the wipe process.

If the employee backed up her iPhone's data to her computer or another location with iTunes, then once your employee buys a new iPhone personally or receives one from the company, have her connect her new iPhone directly to her computer. Once she does, iTunes will appear on her computer screen so she can restore her old iPhone data to her new iPhone.

Finding Security Apps in the App Store

If you want to shop for security apps within the Apple App Store, but you aren't sure which ones are supported by your MDM provider, you don't need to use your own iPhone, iPad, or even the Web to open and peruse the App Store. Within the SimpleMDM website, you can search for security apps that work with SimpleMDM. Here's how:

1. Click or tap Apps in the menu on the left side of the webpage.

2. Click or tap the Add App button.

3. Click or tap Apple Store App in the drop-down menu.

4. In the Add Apple Store App webpage, type "security" (without the quotes) in the Search Terms box.

5. Select the store country from the Store drop-down list if necessary.

6. Click or tap Search.

A list of security apps for the iOS platform that are compatible with SimpleMDM appears on the webpage shown in Figure 2-4.

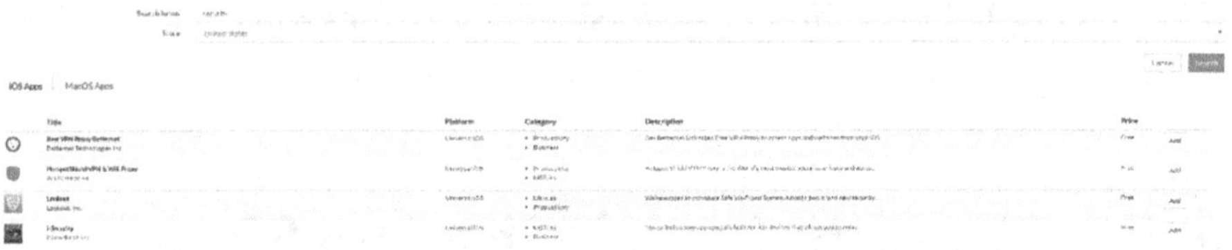

Figure 2-4. *The apps are listed by title, platform, category, description, and price*

You see some products with recognizable company names including McAfee, Symantec, and Avast. All the apps are free, so you can download an app to your own company or personal iPhone and test it before you distribute it to the rest of your employees' iPhones.

Backing Up with iCloud and iTunes

If you're comfortable having your employees back up their iPhones to Apple's iCloud servers using iTunes, they can do this as they would if the iPhones were not managed. iCloud and iTunes are good backup resources because of the security features built into both apps.

iCloud encrypts data from the iPhone while the files are in transit to Apple's iCloud servers, and most stored information in iCloud is also encrypted. The only data not encrypted on iCloud servers is your iCloud Mail account, but this is only a concern if your company and/or your employees use iCloud Mail as one of your email accounts.

Tip   You can learn more about iCloud Security on the Apple Support website at `https://support.apple.com/en-us/HT202303`.

What's more, iTunes opens automatically when you connect your iPhone to your Windows PC or Mac, and then it immediately begins synchronizing and backing up your iPhone.

Backup to iCloud

Within the Backups area of the iTunes window shown in Figure 2-5, iTunes backs up to your computer by default. Click the iCloud button.

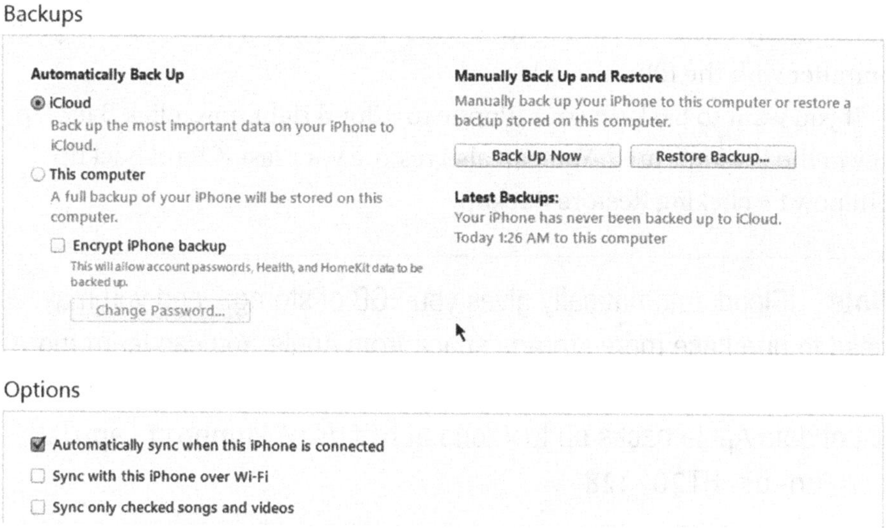

Figure 2-5. *The iCloud button appears at the top of the Automatically Back Up section*

iTunes backs up the "most important data" on your iPhone to iCloud; this includes the following:

- App data

- iMessage, text (SMS), and MMS messages

- iPhone settings

- Photos and videos

- Ringtones

- The organization of your Home screens and apps

- Your call history

In the Latest Backups section, you'll see when you last backed up your iPhone to iCloud and to your computer. Within the Options area directly underneath the Backups area, the Automatically sync when this iPhone is connected check box is checked by default, which means your computer automatically backs up your iPhone when you connect the iPhone to your computer with the iPhone cable.

If you want to back up your iPhone to iCloud right now, click Back Up Now in the Backups area. You can also restore your last iCloud backup right now by clicking Restore Backup.

Note   iCloud automatically gives you 5GB of storage, and you may need to purchase more storage space from Apple. You can learn more about buying more iPad storage from Apple as well as a complete list of data Apple backs up to iCloud at `https://support.apple.com/en-us/HT207428`.

Backup to a Computer

You can use iTunes to back up almost all data stored on your iPhone to your computer. What's more, you can save an encrypted copy of your iPhone data to your computer, which saves the rest of the data stored on your iPhone that a regular backup won't store: your account passwords as well as Health and HomeKit app data.

In iTunes, click the This Computer button if it's not selected already. The Latest Backup section shows when you last backed up to the computer. As with iCloud, you can back up now by clicking Back Up Now or restore your most recent backup now by clicking Restore Backup.

After you click the This Computer button, click the Encrypt iPhone Backup check box. In the Set Password window shown in Figure 2-6, type your encryption password in the Password and Verify Password boxes. When you're done, click Set Password to close the window.

Figure 2-6. *The passwords in both boxes must match before you can click the Set Password button*

You can change the password by clicking the Change Password button and then typing your new password in the Set Password window.

Tip   Before you decide to implement an iTunes backup policy, be sure that all employees' computers have the latest version of iTunes installed so everyone can use the same features.

Unfortunately, you can't manage iTunes with SimpleMDM or any other MDM solution. So before you start backing up each iPhone to a computer, you should set a policy for users to back up regularly. Consider these parameters as you create your policy:

- The iPhone should be connected to the computer via the iPhone USB cable whenever the employee is in the office.

- The This Computer button in the Backups area is selected.

- The Encrypted iPhone Backup check box is checked, and the encrypted password is set by the user.

- The encrypted password is shared with you in your role as the IT administrator in case there's a problem restoring an encrypted backup.

- The encryption password should be changed on a schedule you set.

- The Automatically sync when this iPhone is connected check box cannot be unchecked for any reason.

Of course, you can't monitor all employees to ensure that they're following these backup policies. If you think such policies would be too hard for both you and your employees to manage with their own iPhones, your only other option is to give them company-owned iPhones that are supervised in your MDM system.

Setting Up Supervision Mode

Supervision is a feature in iOS that allows you to install and manage apps, restrict access to apps, and control what employees can view on their iPhone (such as certain webpages), all without the user's permission.

Supervision management is offered by many MDM providers, including SimpleMDM. It's best to start the supervision process with one company iPhone so you can set it up the way you want before you push that configuration to the rest of the iPhones you manage.

Caution   It's not recommended to supervise iPhones owned by your employees, because they likely won't appreciate having little control over how they can operate their iPhone 24 hours a day. What's more, supervision removes all existing apps and data from the affected iPhone. You can't get those apps and data back until you turn off supervised mode, which restores the phone to its normal state.

The following security features are available to you in supervised mode:

- A web content filter

- The ability to prevent syncing with the cloud

- The ability to turn off customizations such as wallpaper and keyboard shortcuts

- Block passcode modifications

- The ability to set the background and lock screen

- Push new apps to an iPhone without the employee's knowledge

- Manage app installation on the iPhone including blocking configuration changes

- The ability to stop automatic app downloads

- Always-On VPN (you'll learn more about VPN in Chapter 3)

- The ability to block specific apps from being used, including these:

  - Game Center

  - iBookstore

  - iMessages

  - News

  - Apple Music

Add Devices to DEP

Before you place your iPhone(s) in supervised mode, you must assign your iPhones in Apple's Device Enrollment Program (DEP) website. (Some iPhones can't be assigned to DEP, which you'll learn about later in this chapter.) Here's how to check the list of devices and add new iPhones:

1. Open the Apple DEP website at `https://www.apple.com/business/dep/`.

2. Click or tap Registered Users Login on the webpage.

3. In the Deployment Programs webpage, type your DEP username and password.

4. Click or tap Sign In.

5. In the Verify Your Identity webpage, select the phone number to send the verification code. If you only have one phone number, the number is selected automatically.

6. Click or tap Continue.

7. Check the device you used to send the verification code and then type the code numbers into the Verification Code boxes.

8. Click or tap Continue.

9. In the Deployment Programs webpage, click or tap Get Started.

10. In the menu on the left side of the webpage, click or tap Manage Devices.

11. In the Manage Devices screen (see Figure 2-7), click or tap the Serial Number, Order Number, or Upload CSV File button. The button you click or tap depends on the information you received from Apple or your cellular provider:

    a. If you want to enter the default serial number, type the iPhone serial number into the box. If you enter more than one iPhone, separate the serial numbers with a comma.

    b. If you click or tap the Order Number button, the Apple order number(s) for the iPhone(s) you purchased appear in the list.

    c. If you downloaded a CSV file from Apple or your cellular provider that contains your device information, click or tap the Upload CSV File button and then click or tap Choose File to open the CSV file.

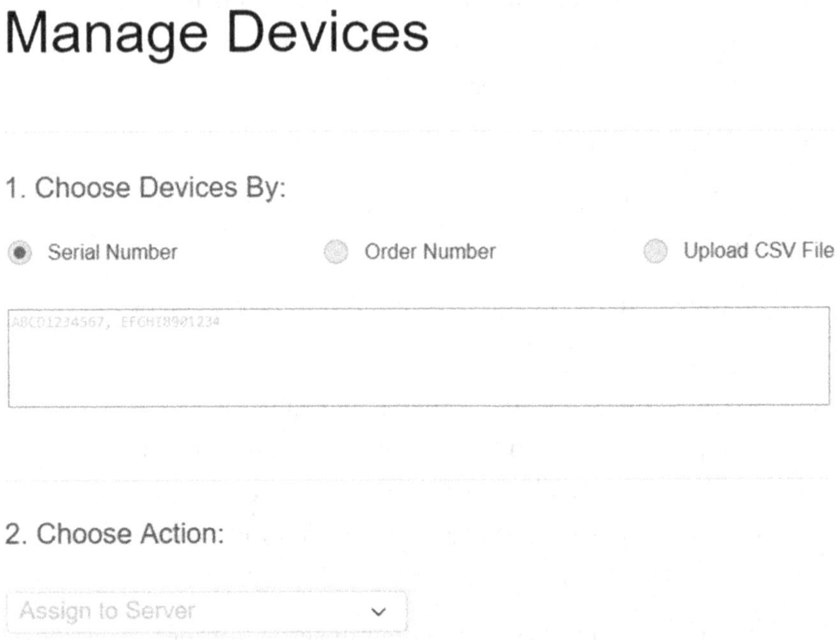

Manage Devices

1. Choose Devices By:

⦿ Serial Number   ◯ Order Number   ◯ Upload CSV File

ABCD1234567, EFGHI8901234

2. Choose Action:

Assign to Server   ⌄

Figure 2-7. *The Serial Number button is selected by default*

Tip   You can find the iPhone serial number by logging into your iPhone, tapping Settings in the Home screen, tapping General, and then tapping About. The serial number is listed in the About screen.

---

12. In the Choose Action section, the Assign to Server option is selected by default. Leave this option selected.

13. Click or tap Choose MDM server and then tap the MDM name in the drop-down list.

14. Click or tap OK.

The added iPhones appear within the Manage Devices list, which means you can manage your iPhone(s) within the DEP website as well as perform more tasks in your MDM, such as supervision.

Add Devices in Apple Configurator

Some iPhones, especially those purchased from cellular providers, cannot be assigned to DEP. In this case, when you add your serial number and assign it to your MDM, a window appears on the screen that says DEP couldn't assign your devices and includes a link to download a CSV-format file you can open to view the reason the iPhone couldn't be assigned, such as "not accessible."

Fortunately, you have another option: You can supervise iPhones using Apple's free Configurator app. The caveat is that this app runs only on Mac computers that run the High Sierra version (or later) of macOS, the Mac operating system. If you don't have a Mac already, then you have two options: manage your iPhone(s) in unsupervised mode, purchase company iPhones directly from Apple so you can assign them in DEP, or buy a Mac.

Caution   Unlike the Apple DEP website, you can only add one iPhone at a time to the Configurator app because the app requires you to connect the iPhone to your Mac using the iPhone USB cable.

How Do I Buy a Mac?

If you've decided that you need to supervise phones purchased from a cellular provider that cannot be assigned to the DEP website, you have several options when it comes to buying a Mac:

- Purchase a Mac Mini, Apple's smallest Mac computer, which costs $499 for the base model. The Mac Mini requires you to connect your own peripherals to use the computer. As of early 2018, the Mac Mini has not been updated since 2014 but is still sold and supported by Apple. The computer also uses the latest version of macOS, High Sierra, so you'll have no trouble using Configurator on the Mac Mini.

- You can purchase one of the MacBook laptop computer models to manage your iPhone(s) in DEP in your own office or when you take the MacBook with you when you visit another company office. The drawback is that you will also have to purchase a USB-C to USB connection adapter for the MacBook or MacBook Pro because those models only come with one USB-C connector port, not a standard USB port used by an iPhone cable.

- You can purchase a desktop iMac to use as one of the computers (or the only computer) you use in your office.

Now that you know your options, you can make your case to management for the option you think is best for the company.

Add Your iPhone

Once you have your Mac Mini, MacBook, or iMac ready to run
Configurator, download Apple Configurator from the Mac App Store.
After you install Configurator, connect your iPhone to your Mac using the
iPhone USB cable, and then launch Configurator. Now, add the iPhone
into Configurator as follows:

1. Turn your iPhone on and then press the Home
    button.

2. Click on the iPhone photo in the Configurator
    screen.

3. Click Prepare in the button bar as shown in Figure 2-8.

Figure 2-8. *The button bar is at the top of the Configurator window*

4. In the Prepare Devices window, keep all the settings in the window to prepare the device with manual configuration, and then click Next.

5. The server you're connected to within Apple DEP appears in the Enroll in MDM Server window. Click Next.

6. The organization that you registered with in DEP appears in the Assign to Organization window. Click Next.

    The list of features the employee will be asked to set up after Configurator resets your iPhone for supervised mode appears in the Configure iOS Setup Assistant window. For example, by default the employee will be able to set up Touch ID on her supervised iPhone.

7. Keep the default Show All Steps option as it is and click Next.

8. Keep the None network profile as it is and click Next.

9. In the Automated Enrollment Credentials window, type your user name and password into the User Name and Password boxes, respectively, if you're going to log into the MDM system for the first time after you set up your iPhone in Configurator. If you already have an MDM system account, leave the boxes blank.

10. Click Prepare.

Your iPhone resets and the Configurator screen on
the Mac tells you about the steps it's taking to get
your iPhone ready.

Note   If you have already prepared the device, then you see a
window that tells you that the device is already prepared. Click
Stop to stop the preparation process and return to the Configurator
window or click Erase to erase all data on the iPhone and prepare the
device again. If you click Erase, you'll lose all apps and data stored
on that iPhone unless you backed up your data using iTunes or other
online file backup service.

---

11. On your iPhone, go through each setup step until
you have entered your Wi-Fi network password in
the Wi-Fi connection step.

12. After Configurator sets up your device, click the
iPhone photo that shows the Hello screen, which
means the iPhone is ready to be configured. Click
Supervised in the option bar shown in Figure 2-9 to
specify that the iPhone will be supervised.

Figure 2-9. *The option bar appears below the button bar*

Tip   If you want to change the iPhone name in Configurator, click iPhone underneath the photo and then type the new name. When you're done, press Enter. It takes a few seconds for Configurator to apply the new name to the iPhone.

Set Up the Supervised iPhone

Now you or your employee can set up their supervised iPhone. If the employee is setting up the iPhone, give her these instructions:

1.   Press the Home button on the iPhone to open the Apps & Data Screen.

2.   Tap Set Up as New iPhone.

3. In the Remote Management screen, tap Next.

4. In the Touch ID screen, set up Touch ID by tapping Continue; for now, tap Set Up Touch ID Later.

5. Create a new passcode in the Create a Passcode screen as you learned to do earlier in this chapter.

6. In the Apple ID screen, enter the Apple ID email address in the Apple ID box and then tap Next.

7. Type your password in the Password box and then tap Next.

8. Type the verification code you received on another Apple device running iOS or on your Mac.

9. In the Terms and Conditions screen, you can read the terms and conditions for your iPhone (or not). When you're done, tap Agree.

10. After a short while, the Express Settings window appears; tap Continue.

11. In the Apple Pay screen, you can set up a credit or debit card to make payments with your iPhone by tapping Continue; for now, tap Set Up Later in Wallet.

12. In the Siri screen, activate the Siri voice assistant by tapping Continue; for now, tap Set Up Later in Settings.

13. In the App Analytics screen, tap Share with App Developers or tap Don't Share, depending on management's policy about sharing app information with developers. If you're not sure, ask your IT administrator.

14. In the True Tone Display screen, tap Continue.

15. In the Meet the New Home Button, tap Customize Later in Settings.

16. In the Display Zoom screen, tap Choose a View.

17. In the Standard screen, tap Next.

18. In the Welcome to iPhone screen, tap Get Started.

The Home screen appears and the iPhone installs all apps that are required for supervised devices. Once the apps are installed, open the SimpleMDM app in your computer's web browser. In the setup screens, always allow the app to use location tracking so you know where employees are if you need to find them, or where the iPhone is if it's lost or stolen.

Note   The next time you press the Power button on your iPhone, a message appears at the bottom of the lock screen that says, "This device is managed remotely."

Create a New Group for Supervised iPhones

In SimpleMDM, you can create separate groups for different types of iPhones. For example, you may want to have a group for supervised iPhones used by rank-and-file employees and a second group for unsupervised iPhones used by you and other managers. Here's how to create a separate group:

1. Click or tap Devices in the left-side menu if it's not open already.

2. Click or tap Groups.

3. Click or tap the blue Create Group button at the right side of the page.

4. In the Add Group webpage shown in Figure 2-10, type the new group name in the Group Name box.

5. Click or tap Save.

Figure 2-10. *The new group name should indicate that the iPhones inside it are supervised*

Assign iPhones to the New Group

The new group with your selected name appears in the Groups screen. Now assign the iPhone to the new group as follows:

1. Click or tap Devices in the left menu.

2. Click or tap the iPhone name in the devices list.

3. In the Device Details screen, click or tap Settings.

4. Click or tap the Device Group box, which says Default.

5. Select the new group name from the drop-down list.

6. Click or tap the blue Save button under the Notes box.

Change Group Configurations

With the iPhone in the new supervised iPhones group, you can apply different feature configurations for all iPhones within the group.

For example, you can specify the wireless network you want all iPhone users in the group to use. You can also add information to your iPhone users in your group such as email addresses. Configuration information about these features is contained in profiles. In Chapter 3, you'll learn about how to set up a Virtual Private Network (VPN) as an example of how to create a profile.

You can view a list of features and their associated profiles as follows:

1. Click or tap Devices in the left menu.

2. Click or tap Groups under the Devices menu.

3. In the Groups webpage, click or tap the group name in the list.

4. In the Group webpage (see Figure 2-11), scroll or swipe up and down the screen to view all the configuration profile types you can add and change.

Figure 2-11. *Scroll or swipe up and down the screen to view all the profiles you can change*

For each feature, profile information appears in one of three categories: existing settings that you can change, links for adding profile information, and selecting information from a drop-down menu to the right of the feature name.

Existing Profiles

If you already have an existing profile for the feature, all you have to do to set the profile is select it from a drop-down list or click or tap on a check box, such as the check box for a wireless network.

Links to Add Profiles

If you don't have any profiles attached to the feature, you can add one by clicking the link and then adding the profile within the Profiles screen. For example, when you click the Add Email Accounts link, the Profiles webpage appears so you can add the profile by clicking the Add Profile button, clicking the Email Account option in the drop-down menu, and add a new email account in the New Email Account webpage.

Drop-Down Menu Selection

If you have one profile attached to the feature, then the profile name appears in the box to the right of the feature name. If you have more than one profile, click or tap the profile name in the box and then select the new profile from the drop-down list.

If you have no profile attached to the feature, add a profile for that feature by clicking or tapping Configs in the menu on the left side of the screen. In the Profiles webpage, click or tap the Add Profile button to select the profile you want to add from the drop-down menu.

When You're Finished

After you add a profile, return to the Groups webpage as you did earlier in this chapter. Then you'll see your new profile within the Configurations list. When you're done setting up your group configuration, click or tap Save in the bottom right of the webpage. SimpleMDM pushes the new configuration to your iPhone(s).

Change Group Settings

If you want to change the name of your group and/or turn device location tracking on and off for all iPhones in the group, here's how to change your group settings:

1. In the left menu, click or tap Devices.

2. Under the Devices header, click or tap Groups.

3. Click or tap the group name in the list.

4. In the Group Details webpage, click or tap Settings.

5. Change the group name by deleting the name in the Group Name box and then typing a new one.

6. If you don't want to track the location(s) of your iPhone(s) in the group, click or tap the Track Device Location check box (see Figure 2-12).

Figure 2-12. *The Track Device Location check box is under the Group Name box*

7. Click or tap Save in the bottom-right corner of the webpage.

If you turned off location tracking, then you can verify that this feature is off by clicking Devices in the left menu and then clicking Devices under the Devices header. The Device Details screen shows you only the last tracked movements on the map before you turned location tracking off.

Note   You can also set rules for each iPhone by clicking or tapping Rules in the Group Details webpage. However, these rules are only used when direct supervision of an iPhone is not an option. Within the Rules webpage, click or tap the Documentation link to open a new browser tab and read more about how to apply rules and what to do if an employee in your group breaks those rules.

CHAPTER 3

Connect to Your Network Securely

There are three ways to connect to the Internet: through a virtual private network (VPN), a Wi-Fi network, or a data carrier's network that uses 4G cellular connection technology. Your employees may be using one or all these connection types on their iPhones, depending on where and when they're accessing the web.

No matter how your employees connect, you know full well it's your job to ensure that they are connecting securely. Your responsibility is not yours alone: Your employees must have security at top of mind when they're using their iPhones, too. (You'll learn about communicating your policies to your employees in Chapter 5.)

What's more, you can use your MDM service to manage your VPN and wireless connections throughout your network. However, your employees may find that a Wi-Fi connection is too weak and need to use a cellular connection, so if your business works with a cellular carrier, you will learn how to use a cellular connection as securely as possible as of this writing (early 2018).

© Eric Butow 2018

E. Butow, *Pro iOS Security and Forensics*, https://doi.org/10.1007/978-1-4842-3757-1_3

Different Connection Types

iPhones can connect to networks in either of two ways, and you're likely familiar with them:

- The Wi-Fi wireless connection standards were developed by the Institute of Electrical and Electronics Engineers (IEEE) and are promoted by the nonprofit Wi-Fi Alliance, a consortium of companies that develops Wi-Fi technologies and certifies Wi-Fi products.

- 4G is the fourth-generation cellular connection technology that currently provides the fastest connection available using cell phone towers. You may also have heard about LTE in connection with 4G, which is a marketing term that means your connection has better than 3G connectivity speeds but hasn't quite reached the speeds required by 4G (at least 100 megabits per second).

You may know that iPhones are automatically set up to search for networks when you first turn them on. What you may not know is the order in which the iPhone will find networks.

The iPhone starts by trying to find your preferred network—the one you've connected to before and have used most often. If you're using the iPhone for the first time, you don't have a preferred network, so it will look for private, Wi-Fi networks nearby. If it finds none, the iPhone will then search for public Wi-Fi networks like those you find at an airport or coffee establishment. If the iPhone can't connect to a private Wi-Fi network, it will try to connect to the first public Wi-Fi network it finds.

However, some networks are hidden, which means that they don't broadcast their network ID (otherwise known as the Service Set Identifier or SSID) so devices like the iPhone can find them. If your company Wi-Fi network is hidden, you can still push your network information to the iPhones you manage through your MDM service.

Virtual Private Networks (VPNs)

A special type of hidden Wi-Fi network you can manage through your MDM service is a Virtual Private Network (VPN).

A VPN is an encrypted connection that creates secure "tunnels" through a wide-area network (WAN), which connects users across large geographic distances. The Internet is the most popular WAN. These tunnels create a network that seems private on a public WAN: Though you're using the Internet to connect, users of the VPN must log in with a username and password to access the data provided only to users who are logged in.

Even though your iPhone is well protected against malware, your data is not safe when it's traveling through a WAN like the Internet. It's also expensive to create your own WAN when you have the Internet doing the same job. So, with their security features designed to let only the right users in, VPNs are recognized by companies and the computing media as the most secure way to connect over the Internet. This may be old news to you as many companies (and perhaps yours) already use VPNs to communicate between local office networks located in different cities.

You need to install a VPN app on your employees' iPhones before you push your VPN data to everyone. Fortunately, there are many good VPN apps available that you can search for within your MDM app.

Tip   If you don't have a VPN set up, type **how to set up a VPN** into your favorite web search engine and you'll see a list of articles that tell you how to create a VPN. You may need to add more to your search terms to get instructions for your specific operating system, such as **how to set up a VPN mac** to get instructions for Mac computers.

Select and Install a VPN App

Within SimpleMDM, here's how to search for VPN apps that you can push to your employees' iPhones:

1. Click or tap Apps in the left-side menu.

2. Click or tap the Add App button in the App Catalog webpage.

3. Click or tap Apple Store App in the drop-down menu.

4. In the Add Apple Store App webpage, type **vpn** (or **VPN**; the term isn't case specific) in the Search Terms box.

5. Change the country store if necessary by clicking or tapping United States and then clicking or tapping on your country name within the drop-down list.

6. Click or tap Search.

You see a results list of VPN apps for the iPhone (see Figure 3-1), but even though every VPN listed says it's free, that's not entirely true. For example, ExpressVPN requires you to pay a monthly fee, but you can cancel the service at no charge within the first 30 days of use.

Figure 3-1. *Scroll up and down the screen to view the entire results list*

Tip   So, which VPN app should you get? A quick web search for "best iphone VPN free" shows many recommendations. You should use at least two criteria to whittle down your list of candidates. First, check to see if the VPN requires any specific hardware to operate, such as a firewall. Second, try a VPN app on an iPhone to see how well it works with your company VPN before you push the VPN app to all your employees' iPhones.

This list does not include all VPNs that SimpleMDM supports, so you may need to enter more search terms. For this example, I'll select TunnelBear because it's well reviewed, it offers a free basic VPN plan, and it's easy to configure.

I searched for "tunnelbear vpn" (without the quotes) to see TunnelBear VPN & Wifi Proxy at the top of the results list. Now here's how to add it:

1. Click or tap the Add button to the right of the TunnelBear VPN & Wifi Proxy entry in the list. The App appears in the list within the App Catalog webpage.

2. In the left-side menu, click Apps.

3. Under the Apps header in the menu, click or tap Assignment.

4. In the App Assignment webpage, click or tap the Add App button in the Apps column.

5. Click or tap TunnelBear VPN & WiFi Proxy in the drop-down list shown in Figure 3-2.

Figure 3-2. *TunnelBear appears at the bottom of the list because apps are listed in alphabetical order*

6. In the Devices column, click or tap Add Device
    Group and then select the group of iPhones to install
    TunnelBear onto from the drop-down list, or click or
    tap Device to add TunnelBear to a specific iPhone.

7. Click or tap Install Apps.

After a few seconds, an App Installation message appears on the lock
screen(s) on the individual iPhone or your employees' iPhone(s). On the
iPhone, tap the Home button and then tap Install in the App Installation
window to begin the installation process.

When you're finished, the app icon appears on your Home screen.
Tap the icon and begin configuring TunnelBear to connect to your VPN
network.

Manage Your VPN from Your MDM

After you add a VPN app to your iPhone(s), you need to tell SimpleMDM
that you have a VPN and its information is ready to connect with your
iPhone. For this example, I've set up TunnelBear on my PC running
Windows 10 because I want to avoid any potential app conflicts as much as
possible, and I can best do that by using the same app to run the VPN on
my computer and access the VPN on my iPhone.

Add a New VPN Provider

You need to start by telling SimpleMDM all about your VPN provider.
Here's how to add that VPN information:

1. In the left-side menu, click or tap Configs.

2. Under the Configs menu header, click or tap
    Providers.

3. In the Account Providers webpage, click or tap Add Provider on the right side of the page.

4. Click or tap VPN Provider in the Account Providers drop-down menu (see Figure 3-3).

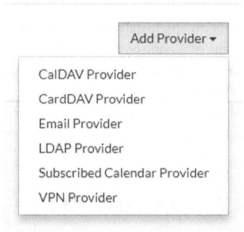

Figure 3-3. *The VPN Provider option appears at the bottom of the menu*

5. In the New VPN Provider webpage, type the name of your VPN in the Name box.

6. If the connection type is not Aruba VIA, click or tap the Connection Type box, which selects that type by default. Then click or tap on the correct connection type in the drop-down list, which in the case of TunnelBear is IPSec (Cisco).

7. Type the hostname or IP address in the Server box.

8. Type the group identifier for the VPN connection in the Group Name box. You may need to check your VPN documentation to see if it already has an identifier.

9. Type the "shared secret" code in the Shared Secret box to authenticate the iPhone with the VPN. You can find this code in the VPN documentation (or you can ask your VPN support if you don't know it).

10. If you want to prompt the user to enter the password on his iPhone every time he accesses TunnelBear, click or tap the Prompt for Password check box.

11. If there is a proxy type, click or tap the Proxy Type box and then click or tap the proxy type in the drop-down menu. TunnelBear does not have a proxy.

12. Click Save (see Figure 3-4).

Figure 3-4. *The New VPN Provider webpage options for an IPSec connection*

Note   The connection type you choose determines the VPN information you need to enter within the New VPN Provider webpage.

The Account Providers webpage appears with the name of the VPN provider in the list. You can change the provider information by clicking or tapping on the provider name in the list and then making your changes in the VPN Provider webpage.

Connect the VPN to Your iPhone

Now that you see the VPN account, here's how to connect the VPN account to your iPhone(s):

1. Click or tap Devices in the left-side menu.

2. Click or tap the device name in the Devices list.

3. In the Device Details screen, click or tap Accounts.

4. Click or tap Add Account in the Accounts drop-down menu.

5. Click or tap VPN within the drop-down menu.

6. In the New VPN Account webpage, type the name for the VPN account in the Name box (see Figure 3-5).

Figure 3-5. *The name of the VPN is the name for the account shown on your iPhone*

7. In the VPN Providers box, type the name of the VPN provider.

Tip   If you'd rather not type the VPN provider name, click the Manage Providers button and then select the providers in the Account Providers screen before you proceed to Step 8.

---

8. Type your VPN username in the Username box.

Tip   If you want to be certain that the password is correct, show your password on the screen by clicking or tapping Reveal under the password box.

---

    9.   Click or tap Save.

The VPN appears in the Device Details webpage accounts list. You can change the VPN account information by clicking or tapping on the VPN name in the list and then making your changes in the VPN Account webpage.

Push Your Wi-Fi Connection

If your company has its own encrypted Wi-Fi connection, you can push this Wi-Fi connection information to your employees' iPhones so their iPhones will connect to your network automatically, or they can select your Wi-Fi network name easily in the Settings screen.

Configure the Wi-Fi connection in SimpleMDM as follows:

    1.   Click or tap Configs in the left-side menu.

    2.   Under Configs in the menu, click or tap Profiles.

    3.   Click or tap Add Profile.

    4.   Click or tap Wireless Network in the Add Profile drop-down menu shown in Figure 3-6.

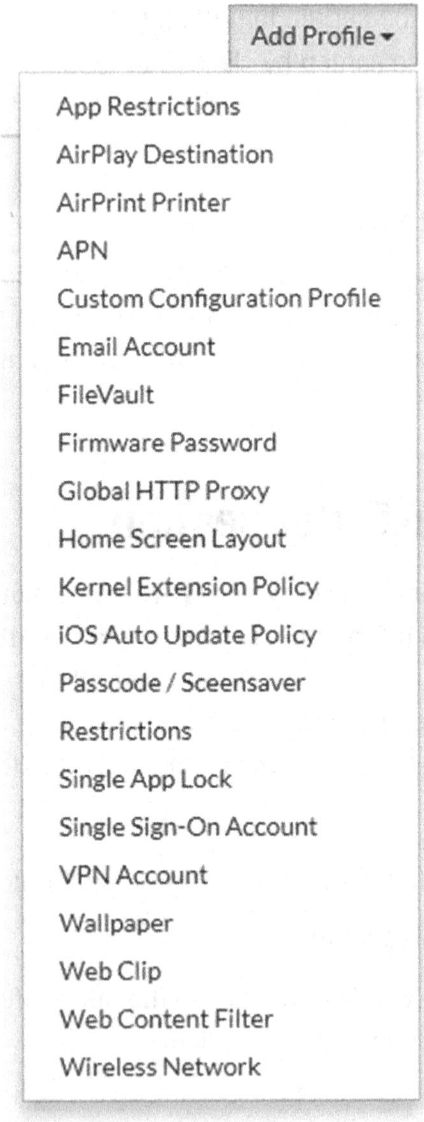

Add Profile ▾

App Restrictions

AirPlay Destination

AirPrint Printer

APN

Custom Configuration Profile

Email Account

FileVault

Firmware Password

Global HTTP Proxy

Home Screen Layout

Kernel Extension Policy

iOS Auto Update Policy

Passcode / Sceensaver

Restrictions

Single App Lock

Single Sign-On Account

VPN Account

Wallpaper

Web Clip

Web Content Filter

Wireless Network

Figure 3-6. *The Wireless Network option appears at the bottom of the menu*

5. In the New Wireless Network webpage, type the name you want to use for the network in the Name box.

6. Type the network name SSID in the Network Name SSID box if the default name isn't correct.

7. The Security Type box shows the default security type; change it by clicking or tapping the Security Type box and then clicking or tapping a new security type in the drop-down list.

8. Type the password for the network in the Password box. (Show the password on the screen by clicking Reveal.)

9. If there is a network proxy, click or tap the Proxy Type box, which shows the default None option, and then click or select the type in the drop-down menu.

10. Since our goal is a secure network, leave the setting in the Treat as Hotspot 2.0 box as No. Hotspot 2.0 is a standard for public-access Wi-Fi for easier identification of and encryption for public Wi-Fi networking, which you'll learn more about later in this chapter.

11. Click Save (see Figure 3-7).

Figure 3-7. *Your network name and password are included by default*

Your Wi-Fi network name appears in the Profiles webpage list. You can change the network settings by tapping the network name within the list and then make your changes in the Wireless Network webpage.

Keep Your Employees Safe and Connected

To this point, you've learned the basics of creating and connecting a VPN connection to your employees' iPhones, as well as pushing your encrypted Wi-Fi connections to iPhones, through your MDM. Your company may have already made the wireless connection choice for you. If the choice is yours, how do you decide? And if you're accountable to the powers that be, how will you convince them that your decision is the right one?

VPN over Wi-Fi

Whenever possible, use a VPN —not only because it's considered the most secure connection method available, but because people have made progress breaking the WPA2 standard wireless security protocol used in encrypted Wi-Fi networks.

In 2017, Belgian researchers broke the WPA2 protocol by using a method called Key Reinstallation Attacks (`https://www.krackattacks.com/`). Though many computing companies offered solutions to fix the problem in late 2017, it's a reminder that encrypted Wi-Fi technology as of early 2018 is still vulnerable. There are some strategies that both you and your employees can take that will be discussed later in this chapter.

The good news is that the Wi-Fi Alliance has announced WPA2's successor, not surprisingly named WPA3, which will offer stronger encryption and privacy protections, to be rolled out some time in 2018. You may want to keep checking the Wi-Fi Alliance website (`https://www.wi-fi.org`) often to find out when WPA3 network routers are coming out.

Even when the WPA3 routers are available, it will take a bit of time to find out how well WPA3 is working to keep users safe. So VPNs remain the most secure method of keeping company and employee data safe.

Using Wi-Fi in Public

There may be times when your VPN or encrypted Wi-Fi connection is not available. Possible reasons may include the failure of the web router at your company site, a power outage at your company site, or the VPN app on your iPhone being down for maintenance. In any of these cases, your employees may be forced to use a public network to connect with your company and get work done or learn when the problems will be fixed.

You can only do so much remotely to keep your employees' network connections safe. Your employees also need to be aware of security issues when they connect to the Internet. Here's the information you need to know about when your employees are using their iPhones out and about. Some of this is probably familiar, but it may not be as familiar to your employees as it should be.

Many public Wi-Fi hotspots, such as ones in an airport using the facility's public Wi-Fi network while you wait for your flight to board, aren't secure. That is, if a hacker is in the same airport, that person may be checking to see who's using an unencrypted connection and use tools to monitor your connection without your knowledge so they can get valuable data such as user IDs and passwords.

It's more likely that a hacker will create a counterfeit Wi-Fi network on their computer, so when you or your employee looks at your list of available Wi-Fi networks in the iPhone Settings screen, that fake network has a name that reasonably looks like it's the Wi-Fi network offered by the public place, and it doesn't have the lock symbol to the right of the name in the list, so this fake network also looks like it's public.

A hacker doesn't have to be at the physical location to create the counterfeit Wi-Fi network; the Wi-Fi signal needs only be strong enough for you to see that Wi-Fi network in the list on your iPhone. If you or an employee logs into this network, the hacker can steer you to counterfeit websites (such as one that looks like your bank's site), monitor your social networks, and see who you're calling.

How to Protect Your Employees

The problem iPhones have is that by default, they search for the nearest Wi-Fi network, and in a public place your iPhone may unwittingly connect to a counterfeit network. So, what can you do and tell your employees to do to stay safe while you're using your (or their) iPhones when your networks aren't available? Here are several strategies to consider.

Ask to Join Networks

If you don't want your employees' iPhones to check for Wi-Fi networks automatically, here's how to make your iPhones ask to join a network:

1. Tap Settings in your Home screen.

2. Tap Wi-Fi in the Settings screen.

3. In the Wi-Fi screen, move the Ask to Join Networks slider button (see Figure 3-8) from left to right.

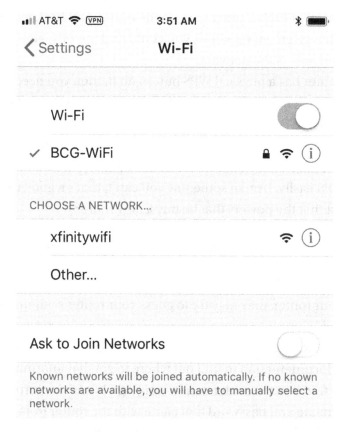

Figure 3-8. *The slider button appears to the right of the Ask to Join Networks menu option*

The iPhone will continue to join known networks, which are networks you've connected to previously. If the iPhone doesn't find any known networks, then the user will have to select a network manually by tapping Other in the Choose a Network section.

Turn Off WPS

WPS, or Wi-Fi Protected Setup, is a common feature on many routers. It is designed to be a security layer for your router and makes it easier for you to connect your router to wireless devices. WPS requires you to enter an eight-digit PIN to gain access to the router, and hackers long ago figured out that given enough time, you could find the PIN, get the router password, and access the network.

If your router has a physical WPS button on it, then you need to disable WPS. However, even the lack of a WPS button doesn't mean that you don't have it. You should confirm that WPS is disabled by consulting your router documentation (if necessary) to access your router's IP address and open your admin settings webpage. Within that webpage, you should be able to disable WPS easily. (And if somehow you can't, that's a good reason to politely insist that the powers that be buy a new router.)

Change Your Router Login Information Often

Hackers know about how to log into routers, too, and if they're close enough to your router, they may try to guess your router's admin username and password.

If you've never checked your router's password, you should check your router documentation to find out where to get that information. (You'll likely find it in the router admin webpage.) Don't be surprised if the generic username and password that came with the router from the factory are easy to guess like "admin" and "1234," respectively.

You should change both your router username and password on a regular basis to make sure that hackers—or even an employee who wants to cause the company harm—have a much harder time gaining access. And it should go without saying that your written admin username and password must be stored in a safe, hard-to-access place.

Ensure Legitimacy or Turn Off Wi-Fi

In a public place where you can ask employees about their network, such as a coffee shop, ask them if their Wi-Fi connection uses Hotspot 2.0, which not only validates correct websites automatically, it also encrypts the public Wi-Fi network with the WPA2 protocol.

If you get a blank stare in response to the Hotspot 2.0 question, ask the employee which Wi-Fi network name they use for their network is the correct one, and then select that network on the iPhone.

Some retail companies, like Starbucks, incorporate some protection. Starbucks uses a login screen that asks you to either tap a button to confirm their terms and conditions or log into their network by entering your contact information.

Many cities offer public Wi-Fi services in cooperation with local or national Internet service providers (ISPs), or some ISPs like Comcast offer public Wi-Fi services, and there is no way to confirm that the public Wi-Fi service website your employee sees is legitimate or has been duplicated by a hacker for nefarious purposes.

If you know your employees will find themselves away from the security of your own VPN or your encrypted Wi-Fi network, you may have some research to do to find out where your employees go and approve certain public Wi-Fi networks, such as those networks you know use Hotspot 2.0.

There's also the zero-tolerance option: Make it policy for employees to turn Wi-Fi off on their iPhones until they can safely access your company network. However, it's impossible to ensure that employees will adhere to the policy, so proper training is essential to make this policy work.

Manage Your 4G Connections

Your company may be paying a cellular provider to access its network because it has employees who go out of Wi-Fi range regularly and need the security of a cellular network to stay connected—provided they're in the cellular provider's coverage area. iPhones contain the Wi-Fi Assist service that's turned on by default. If your Wi-Fi connection is weak, then Wi-Fi Assist will automatically switch the connection to your cellular network so you stay connected.

Tip   There are some limits to what Wi-Fi Assist can do with apps and data roaming that you may want to transmit to affected employees. View the most recent caveats and information from Apple at `https://support.apple.com/en-us/HT205296`.

As of this writing, 4G networks (with or without LTE) provide a more secure connection than public Wi-Fi (without Hotspot 2.0) because 4G connections are encrypted. What's more, you have another strong argument to convince higher-ups to invest in a VPN: You can use a VPN on both cellular and Wi-Fi networks.

Therefore, if your employee is using the VPN on a Wi-Fi connection and her Wi-Fi connection fades out, she can continue to use the VPN on the cellular network. When the Wi-Fi signal becomes stronger, the connection switches back to Wi-Fi. And her security is just as strong with both connection types.

Note   If you haven't done so already, talk with your cellular provider about the security of its network versus use of your encrypted Wi-Fi network to see which option is better for security.

CHAPTER 4

Creating Policies

The previous chapter discussed network connection situations that you and your employees may encounter with your iPhones and the security considerations for each. Once you've made your decisions about iPhone security to ensure that your company data is safe, you need to set iPhone management policies in three key areas.

The first is to determine whether your company will supply company iPhones and require them for work use or will allow employees to use their personal iPhones with company data. Each solution presents its own policy challenges. For example, you will be limited in how you can manage an employee's personal iPhone to ensure that their personal data stays private.

Next, you need to determine who is going to be responsible for managing employees' iPhones if you're not available. What's more, other users (like your CEO) may want to log into your MDM system to see how employees are using their iPhones. You need to create provisioning policies for adding users to your MDM.

Finally, you need to create policies for what happens if a company or personal iPhone is lost or stolen. One part of your policy needs to cover using your MDM to protect your data, such as locking and wiping an iPhone remotely as discussed in Chapter 2. However, you also need to determine if your policies will include protection plans from Apple, insurers, and perhaps wireless carriers for loss, theft, and damage.

© Eric Butow 2018
E. Butow, *Pro iOS Security and Forensics*, https://doi.org/10.1007/978-1-4842-3757-1_4

Your business may have a need for creating iPhone policies based on situations not covered in this chapter. But no matter your situation, as long as you are careful and thorough in creating policies before you communicate them to your employees, the less stressful your life will be.

Note   You'll learn more about communicating your policies to employees and your bosses in Chapter 5.

Company vs. Personal iPhones

No matter how big or small your company is, you have to decide whether to purchase iPhones for your company through either a carrier or Apple or have employees use their personal iPhones to manage company information.

As you create your company policy to communicate to your employees and perhaps your bosses, here's a recap of the security issues involved with each approach as well as some related business issues that you may not have considered.

Company iPhones

If you purchase iPhones through your company, you have more flexibility to operate and manage the phones each employee has. That gives you the most control over how your employees are using their phones, from the types of apps they can use to the networks they can access, by using supervised mode in your MDM system.

What's more, you can install apps on your company iPhones that track what your employees do on those iPhones. These apps not only include expense tracking to make sure that your employees are spending company money wisely, but also track your employees' time and location.

Some messaging apps, like the popular Slack app, also monitor all communications, public and private, within those apps. There are also apps for tracking calls.

Establishing company iPhones requires policies that should include at least the following information:

- Who is going to manage iPhones.

- Which apps are allowed and which are not allowed.

- The process for installing new apps onto iPhones.

- How to add and change professional voicemail greetings.

- If employees can use company iPhones to make personal calls.

- Employee responsibilities including when they are expected to be available to receive work communications on their company iPhones.

- If you monitor messages and calls, detail when you will do so and why.

- Instructions for sharing data between iPhones and the network.

- Requirements for backing up data.

- What happens if an iPhone is lost or stolen.

- What will happen if the employee engages, or tries to engage, in mischief using the company iPhone.

- What happens to company iPhones if the company is involved in litigation (which I'll talk about in the next section about using personal iPhones).

- The process for upgrading current iPhones to newer models.

The MDM system you select will determine how much flexibility you have in meeting your policy needs. It's also highly likely that your employees will bring their personal iPhones to work as well as their company phones, so you will likely have to spell out in your policies when (and perhaps how often) employees can use their iPhones on the job.

Personal iPhones

If you're thinking that your life will be easier if you allow employees to use their personal iPhones for business use, there are three issues you need to know about: privacy, litigation, and stipends.

Privacy

Using MDM systems with personal iPhones may require doing so in unsupervised mode. If you decide you want to put employees' personal iPhones in supervised mode or add apps that allow you or other authorized employees (like the owner) to view activity on employees' iPhones, you'll likely be inundated with complaints over invasion of privacy.

You may also be further limited in what you can do in unsupervised mode. For example, employees may also complain about privacy if you decide to add or remove apps from anyone's iPhone without notice.

Litigation

Attorneys and companies have discovered that if the company is involved in a legal dispute, whether it's civil or criminal, the company's phones and any other computing devices are likely to be confiscated for examination during an investigation.

If your employees use their iPhones for any work-related activities, then investigative teams will take those iPhones and will get the legal permission they need to gain access to all the data on their phones for an uncertain period—if they're returned at all.

Phone Stipends

Your employees may want the company to cover part of their monthly personal phone bill for using their iPhone at work. This payment is called a phone stipend.

A phone stipend must not be offered without rules. For example, employees must be responsible for any costs incurred from damage, loss, theft, and confiscation in a legal case. Some of the policies you set for company iPhones may apply to a personal iPhone, such as requiring the employee to record a professional voicemail greeting that must be approved by you and/or a designated manager.

Your company may decide to make phone stipends a voluntary program: if an employee abides by the rules, they will be eligible for the stipend. For example, you or someone designated by the company may check employees' phones without warning to confirm that they're adhering to the program, which may cause some employees not to participate.

Provisioning Policies for User Management

You may create policies for employee iPhone use with one or more managers in your company—perhaps even the owner or CEO. There is a separate policy that you will also need to discuss with management: Who gets access to the MDM and how much access does each user get?

The policy that answers this question is provisioning, which generally means the company-wide deployment, configuration, and management of technology resources. As applied to MDM systems, provisioning allows you to create new user accounts easily, determine the roles each user has, and change those roles as needed. For example, if you have an assistant, then you may want to give that person a full management role in the MDM while you're on a well-deserved vacation but change the assistant's role when you return to work.

As you create policies for using iPhones, you should also talk with management and any other people in the company (such as the aforementioned assistant) who will need to have access, and once management (or the owner) signs off on the provisioning policy, you can begin adding roles and users to your MDM system.

Adding Roles in SimpleMDM

The only role available by default is Administrator, which allows you to perform all tasks in the system, including these:

- Manage users and their roles.

- Reset the API key for your account; this key is a secret access key that SimpleMDM gives you so you can access your account.

- Change configurations such as app assignments to iPhones.

- Take remote actions on an iPhone such as wipe or lock it.

- View and update your billing details from SimpleMDM.

Here's how to add and set roles in SimpleMDM:

1. In the menu on the left side of the webpage, click or tap Settings.

2. Under the Settings header in the menu, click or tap Users.

3. In the User Management webpage (see Figure 4-1), click or tap Roles.

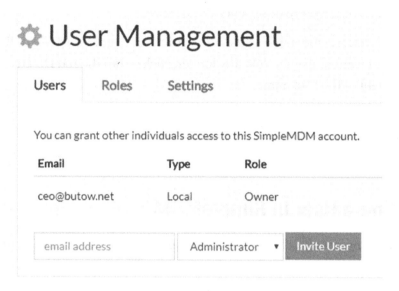

Figure 4-1. *The list of users shows the email address, account type, and role*

4. The Roles page shows the Administrator role in the list; click or tap Add Role at the right side of the screen.

5. In the New User Role screen shown in Figure 4-2, type the role name in the Name box.

Figure 4-2. *The five function check boxes are checked by default*

89

6. Click or tap on the checkboxes underneath the name box to turn off access for those functions.

7. When you're done, click or tap Save.

Now you see the name of the role within the User Management list. If you don't want to use the role any longer, click or tap the red Delete button to the right of the role name.

Note   You can't delete the Administrator role.

Adding a User in SimpleMDM

Now that you've added user roles, it's time to add a user and assign them a role as follows:

1. In the left-side menu on the webpage, click or tap Settings.

2. Under the Settings header in the menu, click or tap Users.

3. In the User Management screen, type the email address of the person you want to invite in the Email Address box.

4. If you don't want the person you're inviting to have an Administrator role, click or tap the Administrator box and then click or tap the role for the user in the drop-down list (see Figure 4-3).

5. Click or tap Invite User.

⚙ User Management

| Users | Roles | Settings |

You can grant other individuals access to this SimpleMDM account.

Email	Type	Role
ceo@butow.net	Local	Owner

| email address | Administrator ▼ | **Invite User** |

| Administrator |
| Power User |

Figure 4-3. *The area to invite users appears under the list of account users*

Setting Advanced User Security Options

The security of your MDM system is just as important as the safety of your employees' iPhones. In SimpleMDM, the default security procedure for logging into your administrator account is the typical username and password that you created after you first set up the system.

If you or your company requires the most stringent authentication possible for all apps it uses, you can either set two-factor authentication or use SimpleMDM with a third-party identity provider app.

Establishing Two-Factor Authentication

Two-factor authentication means you use two different means of accessing your account on an app. In SimpleMDM, two-factor authentication means that you first type in your password when you access the website.

91

Next, you need to finish authenticating your account by typing a code into your system from an app that provides authenticator codes for this purpose. Google Authenticator is a popular authenticator app that you can download from the App Store to your iPhone for free.

Caution   If you're using Single Sign-On (as you'll learn about in the next section), two-factor authentication is disabled automatically.

The following instructions require you to install Google Authenticator so you can require two-factor authentication to log in, and then log into SimpleMDM with Google Authenticator as follows:

1. In SimpleMDM, click or tap Settings in the left-side menu.

2. Under the Settings header, click or tap Users.

3. In the User Management screen, click or tap Settings.

4. Within the Two Factor Authentication section, click or tap the Require Two-Factor Identification check box.

5. Click or tap Save as shown in Figure 4-4.

Figure 4-4. *The Save button appears to the right of the Require Two-Factor Authentication check box*

6. Sign out of SimpleMDM by clicking or tapping your company name or photo in the upper-right of the webpage and then click or tap Sign Out in the drop-down list.

7. Open the Google Authenticator app on your iPhone and instruct the app to scan a barcode, and then activate your iPhone camera if necessary.

8. Move your iPhone screen over the QR code on the SimpleMDM Enable Two-Factor Authentication webpage on your computer or tablet screen.

9. The Authenticator app displays the six-digit authentication code on the screen.

10. In the Enable Two-Factor Authentication webpage, click or tap Continue.

11. Type the six-digit authentication code in the Authenticator app into the 6-Digit Security Code box within the Enable Two-Factor Authentication webpage.

Tip   The authentication code appears in the Authenticator app screen for 30 seconds. Then the code changes. The code number changes to red when it will change within the next four seconds, so instead of rushing to add the soon-to-expire code, it's less stressful to wait for the new code to appear.

---

12. Click or tap Enable in the Enable Two-Factor Authentication webpage.

13. Close the Authenticator app on your iPhone.

The User Settings webpage appears in SimpleMDM so you can make a number of user changes, including these:

- Changing your password

- Disabling Two-Factor Authentication

- Choosing when you receive email notifications from SimpleMDM

- Subscribing or unsubscribing to the SimpleMDM newsletter

- Deleting your SimpleMDM account

You can also return to the Devices screen by tapping the SimpleMDM logo in the upper-left corner of the webpage.

When you log into SimpleMDM in the future, you won't have to scan the QR code every time you log in. All you have to do after you enter the username and password is open your authenticator app on your iPhone and then type the authenticator code into the Security Code box within the SimpleMDM login webpage.

The next time you sign out, SimpleMDM remembers the authentication code as long as your browser remains open. So, when you sign in again, all you have to do is type your username and password.

Using Single Sign-On

If your company uses a number of web apps, you may be logging into all those apps from one third-party authenticator app. You can add SimpleMDM to this authenticator app so you can log into SimpleMDM from your preferred authenticator app.

Here's how to activate Single Sign-On and enter your authenticator app information into SimpleMDM:

1. In the menu on the left side of the webpage, click or tap Settings.

2. Under the Settings header, click or tap Users.

3. In the User Management screen, click or tap Settings.

4. In the Single Sign On with SAML section, click or tap the Yes button to the right of SAML Enabled.

Note   SAML, or Security Assertion Markup Language, is the open-source standard for communicating user authentication information on the web.

---

5. In the Identity Provider information section, type the provider information into the four boxes and select the initial user role from the drop-down list if you want; the default role is Administrator.

6. Click or tap Save in the lower-right corner of the webpage.

7. The sign-in information appears in the SimpleMDM information section (see Figure 4-5) so you can add that information into your authenticator app, such as one of the four preferred SimpleMDM apps: OneLogin, Okta, G Suite, and ADFS.

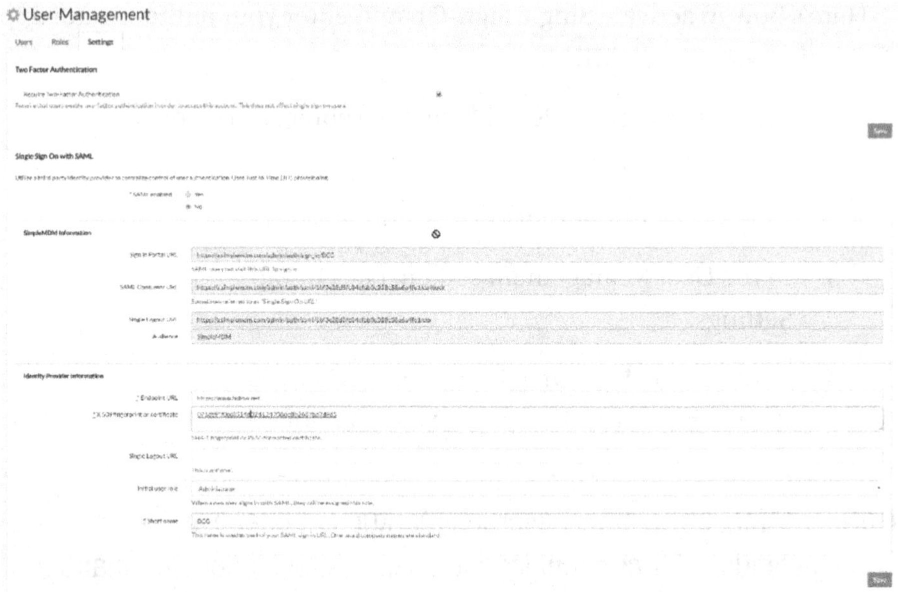

Figure 4-5. *The authentication app information you need appears automatically within the SimpleMDM Information section*

After you set up your authenticator app, close SimpleMDM, restart your authenticator app, and try to log into SimpleMDM within the app.

Tip   If you still can't get your authenticator app to work with SimpleMDM, read the support articles for the preferred app you're using on the SimpleMDM support website at `https://docs.simplemdm.com/category/49-saml-integration-guides`.

Policies for Loss, Theft, and Damage

If your employee iPhones are purchased and supplied by your company, the first thing to do is check with your business insurance company to see if and how well your company iPhones are covered from loss, theft, damage, and natural disasters no matter where your employees are.

Tip   Your insurance company should also be able to tell you what level of coverage is available for employees who use their personal iPhones for work both on company property and off-site.

Apple and other cellular carriers also offer protection plans and insurance if you find that your insurance company doesn't cover iPhone protection as much as you need—or not at all. Your financial manager or other financial personnel will have to research these insurance questions.

As the IT administrator, your financial colleagues may ask you some questions you may have the answers to, such as how the company handles reports of iPhone damage from employees. However, if your business is so small that you do everything plus the bottle washing, set some time aside to work with your insurance company and/or do some insurance shopping.

Before You Start Shopping

Take a moment after reviewing your protection and insurance plans to review your policy about managing damage, loss, and theft of your iPhone. If you don't have a policy, you need to develop one with management to determine how employees will report damaged company iPhones (and personal iPhones if they're covered to some degree by your business insurance) for repair.

For example, you may want to create an online form on your intranet detailing the circumstances that led to the incident, the extent of the physical data or data loss, and anything more that needs to be done to try to recover or repair the iPhone.

Then you would need to find out what steps the IT department would take next, such as:

- Acquiring the damaged iPhone to determine the repair cost and manage the repair process with Apple or your cellular provider.

- If the iPhone is lost or stolen, or even confiscated as part of a legal investigation, the department would take immediate action to lock the iPhone screen and/or wipe the iPhone remotely.

- Determining whether the damaged iPhone will be replaced with the same iPhone model or a different one.

- Arranging for the employee to receive an iPhone replacement as soon as possible and determining if an iPhone would be replaced if it were owned by the company, not a personal iPhone used for work.

- Sending a report to the company financial department for insurance processing.

What's more, you should have the IT department keep track of iPhone damage, loss, and theft, and coordinate that with the financial department when you present your department reports to upper management.

AppleCare and Extended Plans

Apple promotes its AppleCare protection plans when they sell an iPhone so you can minimize the cost of fixing accidental damage. For example, if you're an AppleCare member, Apple will only charge you a $29 service fee for fixing a damaged screen, which is far lower than the cost if you weren't covered.

However, you may balk at the cost of membership: $129 per iPhone to cover an iPhone 8 for up to two years of coverage, and that coverage includes the entire iPhone, battery, and accessories included with the iPhone. Prices for the iPhone 8 Plus and iPhone X are more expensive. You (or your employee) will also have to go to the nearest Apple Store or mail the damaged phone to Apple for repairs.

What's more, Apple limits the number of device incidents during the life of your AppleCare plan. You can view all the latest information about AppleCare, including the fine print, at `https://www.apple.com/support/products/iphone.html`.

If you're purchasing your iPhone(s) through a cellular provider, their representatives may try to push you to purchase an extended warranty that will cover maintenance repair of a damaged iPhone to some degree. You will have to discuss any warranty with the provider and your company management to determine if the warranty gives you enough bang for your company's buck before you sign up.

Insurance

AppleCare or extended warranties from cellular providers only minimize the cost of accidental damage; they don't cover loss or theft. Your insurance company may provide enough coverage that AppleCare is not necessary.

If your insurance won't give you the coverage you need, but you want enough coverage that AppleCare or a cellular provider warranty is unnecessary, here are some leading mobile device insurance carriers to check out.

Worth Ave. Group

Worth Ave. Group (`https://www.worthavegroup.com/`) insures against damage, theft, and a variety of natural disasters including lightning strikes. Your payment depends on the monetary amount you want to cover and the length of the coverage. You can enter this information on their website to get a free quote that will tell you how much the payment and deductible are.

Esurance

Esurance (`https://www.esurance.com/insurance/cell-phone`) is a division of Allstate and provides insurance for loss and theft, damage, and out-of-warranty repairs. Unlike Worth Ave. Group, the amount for coverage is a flat fee paid yearly. As of early 2018, the one-year coverage plan is $79 and the two-year coverage plan is $149, but your deductible varies depending on the type of incident.

Asurion

If you get an insurance plan from your cellular provider, it's most likely one from Asurion (`https://www.asurion.com/phone-insurance/`). Asurion covers iPhones and other smartphones purchased only from cellular providers, but you may want to check the Asurian website anyway to review the services they offer, such as next-day phone replacement.

Every cellular provider has different prices for their insurance plan, so be sure to ask how much the plan costs per month and if Asurion's plans are combined with the provider's extended warranty plan.

Questions to Ask

Here are some questions you need to ask your current or potential insurance carrier for iPhone damage, loss, and theft protection:

- What is exactly covered in the plan(s) I'm looking at? Does it include loss and theft only, or does it also include coverage for damage? And how broad is that damage coverage—will it cover everything from shattered screens to water-damaged iPhones?

- Should you purchase cases for all your iPhones to protect them against drops? Doing so could get you a discount on your insurance rates for those iPhones.

- Is there a deductible, and if so, how much is it?

- How will the company pay for the policy?

- How can you cancel the policy, and are there are any penalties for doing so?

- If you need a replacement iPhone, will it be the same model as the broken iPhone, and when will that replacement arrive?

- Are you limited in the number of replacement iPhones you can get over the life of the policy?

You can get some of this information from online quotes, such as the amount of the deductible. Other information may be harder to get from some companies quickly, which may also factor into your decision. For example, Esurance only allows you to connect with them through a form on their website, but Worth Ave. Group and cellular providers have toll-free numbers you can call.

CHAPTER 5

Communicating About Security

At a minimum, you should communicate your iPhone security policy in a written document, although your company will have to decide how best to present that document. For example, if your company has an intranet, you can make the policy easily accessible to every employee on the intranet home page. An online document also makes it easier to update the document with changes and additions to your iPhone policy.

When you finish developing the policy document, you should introduce it in person not only to reinforce the information in the document, but also to answer any questions from employees. You may want to add some of the questions and answers to your written policy in a "frequently asked questions" section.

Your employees must also be made aware that they have responsibilities of their own to keep their iPhones secure as they use them. Employees will be the targets of email scammers called "phishers" when they're at work just as often as they are when they're at home. Their activities on the Safari web browser may also be tracked by some websites, and employees need to know how to surf the web privately.

Employees are also responsible for managing the privacy settings of their apps since you can't do this remotely with your MDM system. Therefore, you need to give users instructions about how to change these settings in the iPhone Settings screens.

© Eric Butow 2018
E. Butow, *Pro iOS Security and Forensics*, https://doi.org/10.1007/978-1-4842-3757-1_5

Finally, your employees may already know that the iOS operating system and iPhone apps are updated regularly, but with managed iPhones, the responsibility falls on you and your IT staff to ensure that your employees' iPhones are updated regularly and to tell your employees when those updates are coming so they can schedule that time for other activities.

Communicate Your Policies

Hopefully, you have already obtained management approval to create written iPhone usage and management policies—or you'll soon approach management to convince them that creating such policies is necessary for the company's data security.

How you come to create your policy depends on what you and your management decide. For example, management may want you and/or the IT department to create the policy and then have management review it. You'll likely need management approval if you want to create and lead a committee of IT staffers, managers from different departments, and at least one employee in each department to help craft and refine the policies, and then present them to select groups of employees (perhaps by department) to educate them and receive feedback. It's also possible that you may be the only person who develops the entire policy.

No matter how you create your policy, as the IT director, you'll be involved. So, get out your calendar now and set deadlines if necessary, and then set aside time each day to create, refine, and communicate the policies to your employees.

Check Your Existing Policies

Before you begin writing your policy, check to see if you have any other written IT-related policies for the company. An existing laptop computer security policy is especially useful as you develop your iPhone security policy because some of the rules are similar, such as what to do in case your company laptop is lost or stolen.

Your laptop security policy may also expose where both you and your employees are falling short in implementing that policy, and that may give you the opportunity to work on improving the laptop policy at the same time you're working on the iPhone policy. When you're satisfied with your laptop security policy, you can apply what you learned from updating that policy to your iPhone security policy.

If you don't have a written laptop policy, you can use the information in this chapter to create, or ask management to create, related policies for using other company computers and devices after the iPhone policy is complete.

Creating Policy Documents

When you create policy documents, it's best to create and distribute them online, such as through a company intranet, for three reasons:

1. Employees can access the policy document more easily, and employees can also print out sections of the documents that they want to read on paper.

2. It's easier to update when there is new information, and then you can send information about updates to employees via email or your company's messaging system.

3. You can include multimedia files such as audio and video demonstrations, as you'll learn about later in this chapter.

For example, you can use an online help authoring tool such as Adobe RoboHelp or MadCap Flare to create a help system that contains different topics that employees can access by tapping the topic name in the table of contents. Employees can also find terms by clicking links within topics as well as searching through the index and glossary.

Unlike a Portable Document File (PDF) you view in the free Adobe Reader or a similar app, your online help system can incorporate video and audio demonstrations to show employees how to perform certain tasks. Figure 5-1 shows an online help example with the table of contents in the left pane of the window and a multimedia instructional video in the right pane.

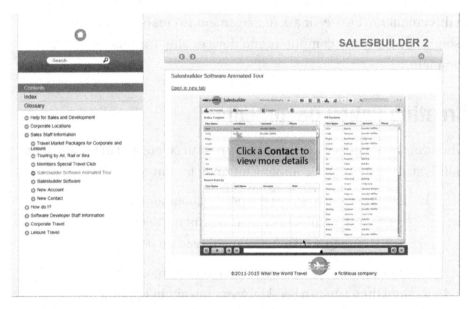

Figure 5-1. *You can play, rewind, fast forward, and pause the video within the right pane*

How you present the policy depends on how your company communicates with its employees. No matter whether you distribute the policy by paper, in a PDF file, in an online help system, or through some other electronic means, you need to answer the following questions before you start creating your policy.

Who is My Audience?

If you have a number of employees who don't know how to use their iPhones very well, then you may have to add more definitions of terms and have more step-by-step instructions to show how to perform actions that will enhance their iPhone security. If you have employees in different countries, you not only need to consider differences in languages, you need to understand how an iPhone works in those countries. In the latter case, you should also have a manager or employee from that country help you craft your policy.

How Much Information Do I Include?

You may want to poll employees or, if there are too many employees to ask, poll managers about how they use their iPhones. Ask them if they do anything to secure them, and if they're familiar with certain terms like phishing, which will be discussed later in this chapter. From that feedback, you can determine how much information should be included in each topic.

You should also create a glossary of terms in your policy that will make it easier for employees to understand what you're talking about. The more an employee knows and understands security terminology, the more likely the employee will help you keep their iPhone secure and report any potential attack to her manager or the IT department as quickly as possible.

What Is the Employee's Responsibility?

It's likely that in your company, it's the IT department's responsibility to tell the employee that even though the department is managing everyone's iPhone to some degree to keep their data safe. However, the company has entrusted the storage of its data (and perhaps a company-supplied iPhone) to the employee, and so the ultimate responsibility for security rests with the employee.

This means the employee is also responsible for reporting any suspicious activity and reporting the loss or theft of the phone as soon as possible. Your policy may include information about the consequences for an employee who fails to meet that responsibility.

How Do Employees Report an Incident?

Once employees have the information they need and knows their responsibilities, how do they report a potential or known security problem? The IT department (including you) and upper management will have to answer important questions, including:

- Will company employees, contractors, or a third-party company manage security incidents?

- Who will handle inquiries and reports from employees during office hours?

- Who will handle inquiries and reports during off hours?

- Can employees access security information from an online system accessible at any time?

- Can employees call a hotline number to report a potential or active incident, and if so, will the hotline be available during a certain period or 24 hours a day?

- Who will log security incidents within the company, and how will that be done?

- Who will review security incidents to determine if changes need to be made to policy and/or device management?

- When will a security incident be considered resolved?

These are just some questions that will help you determine how your company can keep track of a problem, implement a solution, and work as hard as possible to prevent the problem from recurring. You will likely come up with more questions that need to be answered depending on your company's needs that will need to be included in your policy documentation.

How Can Employees Give Feedback?

Employees will have questions about your policy, both when you create the policy document and when the policy goes into effect. If your employees aren't sure how to ask for feedback or how to contact you, here are some suggestions:

- Send a regularly-scheduled email message to all employees about what's happening with IT, and in each message invite people to email as well as call and/or text to a specific number if an employee has questions or issues about IT.

- Have a space on your company intranet to contact the IT department with requests or concerns, either through an email message, with online help desk personnel, and/or by filling out a form and submitting it to the department. You should also include the IT phone number for either the help desk department or the person in the IT department designated to help employees.

- If you create an online policy guide, be sure to include contact information that you can easily find in the same location either in a section of the screen or on every topic page.

Note   If the feedback or suggestion results in an improvement to IT policies or procedures, consider asking the employee to mention your name in a future communication to thank them for their help. Likewise, if your company invites employees to recognize others for their good work, consider submitting that employee's name for recognition.

How Do I Ensure Employee Compliance?

Your company may require that all employees communicate their understanding not only of your IT policy but of all company policies. No matter what your company communication policy is, be sure that the IT policy includes a requirement that employees acknowledge their understanding of these policies so that in case of an incident, you can avoid as much as possible any claims of misunderstanding by the affected employee(s).

To show that employees understand a policy, your company may simply require that the employee sign a written document that states they understand the policy and the consequences for violating it, and then the company places that information in the employee's file. However, some employers may want their employees to take a test, either based on straightforward questions or requiring employees to evaluate different scenarios to demonstrate their understanding of those policies.

You can create these tests in free form creation software such as Google Forms, or create more elaborate tests that also include multimedia examples within dedicated test-creation apps such as Adobe Captivate. After the employee finishes the test online and clicks or taps the Submit button to send to the appropriate (preferably IT) person for evaluation, the IT department can verify to HR and the employee's manager that the employee has passed the test.

If your company doesn't yet have a policy for showing that the employee passed the test, consider including that element in your policy. For example, it could say that each employee who has passed the test will receive a document from the IT department, and a copy of that document will be placed in the employee's file.

Communicating Your Policy

When the iPhone policy is completed and approved, the next step is to communicate it to all employees of your company. The communication method may be a meeting of all employees or, if the company is too large, staff meetings of all the departments in the company.

Before you set your first meeting, be certain to script and rehearse the presentation before you begin. You should practice your presentation either with your IT team, some members of management, or other people you've asked to participate and provide feedback. (The prospect of getting away from the desk for an hour or two may be all the incentive they need to say yes).

Presentation Needs

If you're not sure what information to include in your presentation, here are some ideas to get you started:

- Review the purpose of the policy, how it was put together, why this IT policy is important, and how the policy should be used.

- Demonstrate the types of security issues employees will confront often when they use their iPhones, especially attacks through email and the web. (Information about these attacks will be discussed later in this chapter.) This may be a good opportunity to ask people in the audience to role-play to show what can happen and what the consequences can be to the company and to employees.

- Also use role playing with your audience to show the good things that happens when employees use correct security procedures per the policy document. For example, if your company uses a password manager app (which you'll learn about later in this chapter), then you'll show how easy it is to keep your web passwords safe. You can also demonstrate what happens in the IT department when an employee calls in a suspected or actual threat and how the employee's quick actions help save the company a lot of money— and their fellow employees a lot of stress.

- Tell your audience where they can get the policy as well as any other related information, such as a video recording of the presentation.

- Inform your audience that they need to demonstrate they understand this iPhone policy either through testing, signed agreements, or both. You may want to have your HR manager speak about policies in general and why it's important for employees to understand all company policies and have that information on file.

- Let employees know how to contact you with questions or concerns and encourage them to contact you at any time no matter how small they think their issue may be. The information they give may result in an important change to the policy or a thwarted attack, and the reporting employee may be recognized for their contribution.

You may also get some other presentation ideas from management and your IT staff that is company-specific, such as discussing apps you use on employees' supervised iPhones.

Recording Your Presentation

When you give your presentation, consider recording it on video and make it available on the company intranet so employees can refer to it when they need to. If you're giving several presentations to different departments, consider recording all of them and then choose the recording you feel is the best presentation to show on the intranet.

Recording your video is especially important if your company spans more than one location, because IT departments in those locations can either present that video to employees at their locations or create their own presentations based on yours but include changes to reflect their specific office needs. For example, if you have an office overseas, then it's likely that local IT department will create its own country-specific presentation built from what you have in your presentation.

This presentation does not have to be the only one you use. As you update your policies, you may need to develop more presentations about the updates, although you may decide just to record those presentations, place them online, and alert employees that they need to watch those videos (perhaps by a certain date).

Note   You may need to check with management to ask if they want employees to take a test and/or sign a form that acknowledges that the employee understands the updated policy information and its effects on the company so there is no doubt that the employee is up-to-date on iPhone security matters.

Phishers are Fishing for You

One of the common attacks employees will encounter from the outside world is phishing, which is the practice of sending emails from what looks like a legitimate sender in an attempt to get you to give the real sender confidential information. For example, the phisher hopes to make you click on a link that will open a website that looks like one you normally use but will fool you into entering your user ID and password for their own malicious use.

Phishers will also try to make you click on a link or attachment that will open malware, but fortunately the iPhone's built-in protections make such an attempt more likely on one of your company's computers than on an iPhone. Attempting to fool you into revealing your login information for a sensitive website is the phisher's most effective use of your iPhone to do harm to you and your company.

Emails from phishers can be well-researched to target specific recipients, including people at your company. A phisher may even try to use a name at your company or a client's company, which is easy to find on an About Us page on a company website, to try to trick you and your employees.

Look for the Hooks

Even so, phishers have to include certain hooks that are obvious if you know what to look for. Here are some examples that you should communicate to your employees as part of their training:

- An unfamiliar sender, even if they're from your company or a client company. For example, the message may be from someone the employee has never worked with before and would not work with because the sender is in a different, unrelated department.

- An unfamiliar greeting (like starting the message with formal words like "Dear" or "Hello") or a manner of writing that doesn't read like the person who's sent you email messages in the past.

- A request from the IT department to download an attached file that an employee is not expecting and does not recognize.

- An invitation from another department to click on a link to a webpage that looks like it's from your company and asks you to verify your login information by entering it into the webpage. For example, the message may claim it's from the financial department and asks the employee to enter his bank account information.

- A message from someone the employee knows that claims to be sending him an attachment per his request.

- A lot of grammar and/or spelling mistakes. This is perhaps the most obvious way to spot a phisher, but it may not be if the sender is someone known not to be a great speller. Good phishers also take care to use good spelling and grammar.

- A message with threats and/or urgent requests. The email message may say that the employee needs to install an app to protect immediately against a security threat. This kind of message may be associated with a threat of negative consequences for the employee (like being fired) if she doesn't install the app or provide requested information immediately.

Check and Communicate

Any phisher who is determined and sophisticated enough can succeed in fooling anyone into giving information that will benefit them and harm you, your fellow employees, and the company. So it always pays to be suspicious with all emails you receive. Here are ways employees can protect themselves that you can communicate to them:

- Check the email address of the sender to verify that the email address matches the sender. You can do this in the iPhone Mail app by opening the message and then tapping the sender name at the top of the screen to view the sender's information, including the email address.

- Watch out for any of the following:

    - A message is sent to other people as well as you. If the person who is copied doesn't look familiar, then it's possible the email was sent by a phisher.

Tip   If you can't view the name(s) of the persons copied on the message at the top of the email message, tap Details below the sent date and you'll see the list of people copied in the message in the Cc list. View the email address and other information about a person in the Cc list by tapping on the person's name.

- The subject of the email doesn't look right, such as "As you requested."

- You receive a message with an attachment you aren't expecting, no matter who sent it to you. Even if you receive a message from someone, you may want to confirm that the sender email address is legitimate.

Take care to conclude your discussion by reminding employees that if they find any messages like these on their iPhone, or if there's something else that looks suspicious to them, always contact the IT department either by email, on the intranet, or by phone, or contact their manager for guidance.

Caution   Warn employees not to reply directly to the message, Instead, tell employees to send a separate message to the IT department or the manager about the suspicious email.

Staying Safe Browsing the Web

Your employees can limit the amount of information that websites can detect from within the Safari web browser. On supervised iPhones, you can also block or allow certain websites from within your MDM system.

You should consider adding the following Private Browsing information into a document on your company intranet and give this information in your in-person presentations to show how Private Browsing affects employees' web surfing experience in Safari, and how it improves their browsing security, so they can decide if they want to use Private Browsing or not.

Private Browsing in Safari

The Safari web browser on the iPhone has a built-in privacy setting that you can activate to block some information and functionality within the browser. While Private Browsing is turned on, Safari does not:

- Save any passwords entered into any website.
- Save any record of your browsing history.
- Preserve any search history.
- Allow auto-completion (what Apple calls AutoFill) of saved usernames and passwords.

117

Here's how to turn on Private Browsing:

1.   Tap Safari in the Home page if the Safari app isn't open already.

2.   Tap the Switch Tabs icon in the lower-right corner of the screen.

3.   Tap Private in the Tabs screen, shown in Figure 5-2.

     Private Browsing Mode information appears on the screen so you can read more about it if you want.

Figure 5-2. *The Private option appears in the lower-left corner of the Tabs screen*

4. Tap Done.

5. Tap the Open icon in the bottom center of the
    screen to view a new website in Private Browsing
    mode.

The Safari color scheme in Private Browsing mode changes to black
and dark gray. All websites you visit in Private Browsing mode only appear
in the Tabs screen when Private Browsing is turned on. When you want
to turn off Private Browsing, repeat steps 1–3. The Safari color scheme
changes back to its usual white and gray, and any website you're viewing in
public mode appears on the Tabs screen.

What Private Browsing Won't Block

Private Browsing allows only some cookies to be blocked, but Apple's
engineering division will not divulge why that is or what cookies are
allowed. So, tell your employees what Private Browsing can't do:

- Block a website from viewing your device and behavior
  on the site.

- Keep a saved website bookmark private; all bookmarks
  are available in normal (public) browsing mode.

- Stop monitoring software installed on a company
  iPhone from recording your activity.

- Block websites from viewing your device IP address
  and any data associated with that address.

Note   You may need to include an explanation of what an IP address is and why data is associated with it.

Block All Cookies

Private Browsing will block some websites from adding cookies to Safari to track your activities, but not all. If your employees want to block all cookies, tell them they can activate this setting in the Settings screen as follows:

1. Tap Settings on the Home page.

2. Swipe up in the screen until you see Safari in the Settings list.

3. Tap Safari.

4. Swipe up in the screen until you see Block All Cookies in the list.

5. Swipe the slider button that appears to the right of Block All Cookies from left to right (see Figure 5-3).

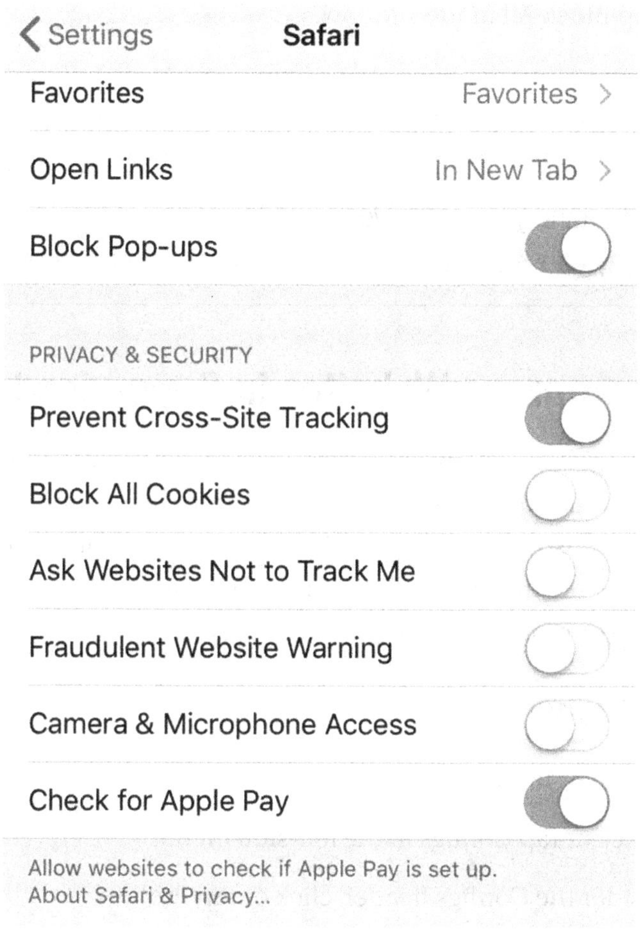

‹ Settings   **Safari**

Favorites	Favorites >
Open Links	In New Tab >
Block Pop-ups	⬤

PRIVACY & SECURITY

Prevent Cross-Site Tracking	⬤
Block All Cookies	◯
Ask Websites Not to Track Me	◯
Fraudulent Website Warning	◯
Camera & Microphone Access	◯
Check for Apple Pay	⬤

Allow websites to check if Apple Pay is set up.
About Safari & Privacy...

Figure 5-3. *When you swipe the Block All Cookies slider button from left to right, the button turns green*

6. Tap Block All in the window.

If you want to turn the Block All Cookies feature off, follow the steps above except that in step 5, swipe the slider button to the left.

Caution   Remind your employees that blocking cookies from all websites may cause some websites to function incorrectly or not at all.

Block or Approve Websites in Supervised Mode

If you're managing company employee website use in supervised mode, then you may want to block certain websites from being used, such as pornography websites. In SimpleMDM, all websites are automatically whitelisted (the technical term for approved). However, it's easy to blacklist (or block) one or more websites.

Blacklist Websites

To blacklist one or more websites:

1. Click or tap Configs in the left-side menu.

2. Under the Configs header, click or tap Profiles.

3. Click or tap the Add Profile button on the right side of the Profiles webpage.

4. Click or tap Web Content Filter in the Add Profile drop-down list (see Figure 5-4).

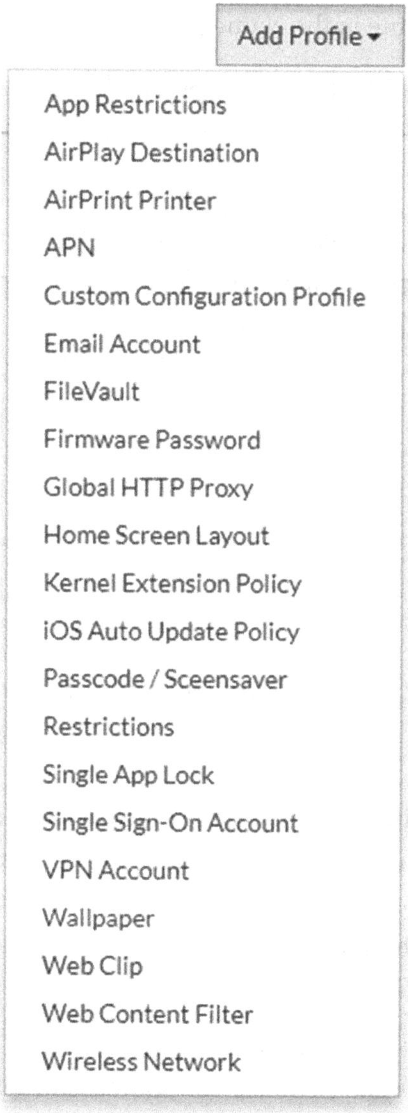

Add Profile ▾

App Restrictions

AirPlay Destination

AirPrint Printer

APN

Custom Configuration Profile

Email Account

FileVault

Firmware Password

Global HTTP Proxy

Home Screen Layout

Kernel Extension Policy

iOS Auto Update Policy

Passcode / Sceensaver

Restrictions

Single App Lock

Single Sign-On Account

VPN Account

Wallpaper

Web Clip

Web Content Filter

Wireless Network

Figure 5-4. *The Web Content Filter option is the second from the bottom in the list*

5. In the New Web Content Filter webpage, type the new filter name in the Name box.

6. The default filter type is blacklist, which means the site won't appear in Safari, so leave this filter type as is.

7. Click Save.

8. If you want SimpleMDM to exempt certain websites from the filter list, click or tap the Enable Auto Filter check box (see Figure 5-5).

Figure 5-5. *The Enable Auto Filter check box appears below the Filter Type box*

9. In the Permitted URLs box, type the website address you want to exempt from the filter. The address must include the http:// or https:// prefix. If you have more than one website address, separate each address with a space.

10. In the Blacklisted URLs box, type the website address you want to block. The address must include the http:// or https:// prefix. If you have more than one website address, separate each address with a space.

11. When you're done, click or tap Save.

Now you see the web content filter within the Profiles list. Test your filter in Safari on a supervised iPhone and see if it works. If it doesn't, or you need to make other changes, you can change the filter by clicking the web content filter name in the Profiles list and then making changes in the Web Content Filter webpage. If the filter change still isn't working, contact SimpleMDM support on the SimpleMDM website for more assistance.

Whitelist a Website

If you have a hidden website with a specific URL that you want to bookmark in Safari, here's how you can whitelist the hidden site:

1. Under the Configs header, click or tap Profiles.

2. Click or tap the Add Profile button on the right side of the Profiles webpage.

3. Click or tap Web Content Filter in the Add Profile drop-down list.

4. In the New Web Content Filter webpage, type the new filter name in the Name field.

5. Click or tap blacklist in the Filter Type box and then click or tap whitelist.

6. Click or tap Save.

7. Tap the Add Bookmark button (see Figure 5-6).

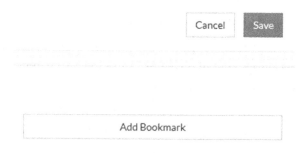

Figure 5-6. *The Add Bookmark button appears below the Cancel and Save buttons on the right side of the webpage*

8. In the New Bookmark webpage, type the website address (with the http:// or https:// prefix), bookmark title, and an optional folder you want to add the bookmark into.

9. When you're finished, click or tap Save.

    The bookmark appears within the Bookmarks sections at the bottom of the Web Content Filter webpage.

10. Tap Save.

The whitelisted filter name appears in the Profiles list. Now you can view Safari on your iPhone, tap the bookmarks you added, and confirm that they go to the whitelisted websites. If they don't, you can change the list by clicking or tapping the filter name in the Profiles list. If that doesn't work, contact SimpleMDM support on their website for more assistance.

Manage Passwords

If your employees log into websites to perform tasks, even if the list of sites your employees can access is limited to your intranet and other whitelisted sites, you may want to install a password manager app that will allow you and your employees to create strong passwords for your websites, manage passwords easily within the app, and not have to remember all your website passwords.

If you decide to install a password manager on your managed iPhones, it's easy to search for the term "password manager" (without the quotes) in the App Store to find a list of password managers that start with the most popular as of this writing, Keeper. Once you decide on a password manager, write and send instructions for using the app (or send a link to the company website page that contains these instructions) to your employees before you push the app to their iPhones.

As with other apps such as a VPN that is meant to secure company data on your iPhone, you need to include information in your employee training about how to use your chosen password manager and why it's important to use it.

Managing App Permissions

As of this writing, there is no way to manage app permissions on an iPhone using an MDM system. Employees must manage permissions for built-in apps (such as Photos) as well as apps that have been installed on their iPhones. Therefore, you will have to send them the following instructions for managing their app permissions.

If you want to see what apps another app has access to, do the following:

1. Tap Settings in the Home screen.

2. Swipe up in the screen until you see Privacy in the Settings list.

3. Tap Privacy.

4. Swipe up and down the screen to view the built-in apps that other apps have access to, and then tap the built-in app name in the list.

If the app you're checking is being used by one or more other apps, then you'll see the name of that other app in the list, as shown in Figure 5-7. (You can still use your iPhone to track your fitness data at work every day if you're so inclined.) Turn off access to the app by the other app by tapping or sliding the slider button to the right of the other app name from right to left.

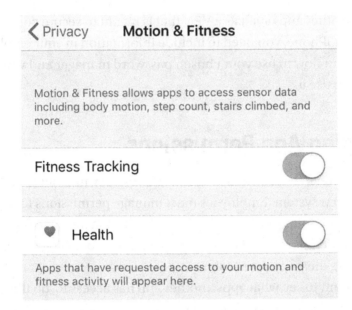

Figure 5-7. *Any related apps that the current app is using appear in the list on the app screen*

If you want to change app permissions for a third-party app that you or the company has installed, open the Settings screen in the iPhone and then swipe up in the screen until you see the app you want to change. When you tap on the third-party app name in the Settings list, you'll see the native iPhone apps, like the Camera app, that you can permit the third-party to use (or not).

Updating iOS and Apps Regularly

SImpleMDM requires you update iOS and installed apps on computers that you manage no matter whether they are supervised or not. SimpleMDM requires that you do this manually, so as part of creating your policy for managing your iPhones, you must determine who is responsible for pushing upgrades to apps and iOS and when those upgrades will be performed.

Unsupervised Mode

In unsupervised mode, you can either push the iOS update or let the iPhone alert the employee that an update is pending through a numerical badge on the Settings icon. For example, 1 in a red circle says there is one issue to attend to, and when you tap the Settings icon you find out the issue is a pending iOS update.

The same is true for apps: You may see a badge in the upper-right corner of the App Store icon. However, the iPhone is set to update apps automatically right out of the box.

Note   Though an individual employee can update iOS and apps from your iPhone, you should make it policy for all iOS and apps on all managed phones to be managed by the IT department. This ensures that all employees have the same iPhone functionality.

Before you can manage iPhone updates through SimpleMDM or any other MDM system, you need to turn off automatic updates for app and iOS updates on each employee's iPhone. Here's how:

1. Tap Settings in the Home screen.

2. Swipe up in the Settings screen until you see iTunes & App Store.

3. Tap iTunes & App Store.

4. In the Automatic Downloads section in the iTunes & App Stores screen (see Figure 5-8), tap or swipe the slider button to the left to turn off automatic downloads for Music, Apps, Books & Audiobooks, and Updates.

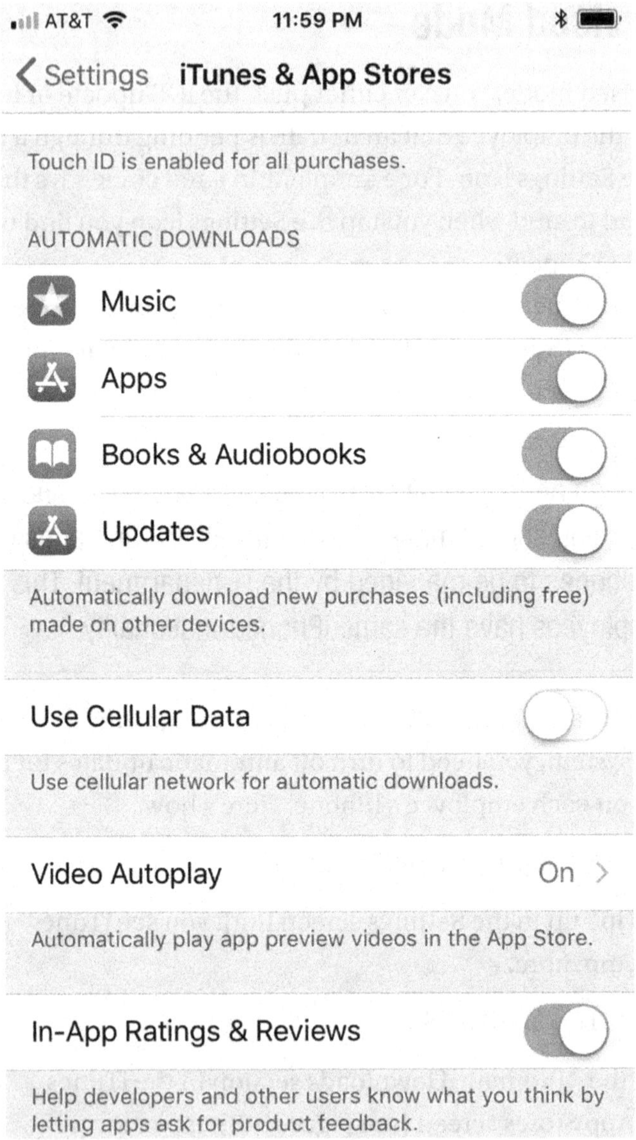

●ıll AT&T 🛜   11:59 PM   ✳ ▬▬

< Settings   **iTunes & App Stores**

Touch ID is enabled for all purchases.

AUTOMATIC DOWNLOADS

⭐ Music   ⬤◯

🅰 Apps   ⬤◯

📖 Books & Audiobooks   ⬤◯

🅰 Updates   ⬤◯

Automatically download new purchases (including free)
made on other devices.

Use Cellular Data   ◯

Use cellular network for automatic downloads.

Video Autoplay   On >

Automatically play app preview videos in the App Store.

In-App Ratings & Reviews   ⬤◯

Help developers and other users know what you think by
letting apps ask for product feedback.

Figure 5-8. *By default, all automatic downloads are on, as shown by*
the green slider buttons

Update from SimpleMDM

No matter whether you're managing unsupervised or supervised iPhones, it's easy to update iOS and app updates within SimpleMDM.

iOS Updates

Here's how to update the iOS version on all your managed iPhones:

1. In the left-side menu, click Devices.

2. Click or tap the check box to the left of the device name you want to add.

Tip   You can select all devices by clicking or tapping the check box to the left of the Device Name column title, which appears in bold text.

---

3. Click or tap the Actions button in the upper-right area of the webpage.

4. Click or tap Update iOS Version (see Figure 5-9) in the Actions drop-down list to begin the update process for all affected iPhone(s).

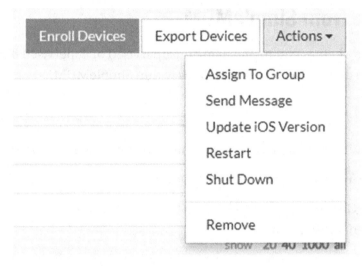

Figure 5-9. *The Update iOS Version option is the middle option within the drop-down list*

5. Tap OK in the window to confirm that you want to update iOS on the selected iPhone.

Now check the iPhone to ensure that it has checked for a new iOS update and has either reported that there is no iOS update (which means you'll have to try again in a few minutes), or you see the upgrade screen so the employee can manage the upgrade process.

App Updates

To update apps in all your managed iPhones:

1. Click or tap Apps in the menu on the left side of the webpage.

2. Under the Apps header, click or tap Assignment.

3. Within the App Group section of the iPhone(s) you want to update, click or tap Add App.

4. Select the app you want to add from the Add App drop-down list.

The apps you're going to update appear underneath the Add Apps box (see Figure 5-10).

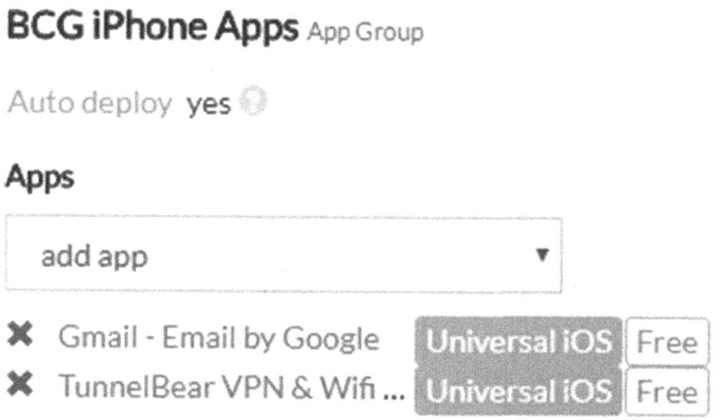

BCG iPhone Apps App Group

Auto deploy yes

Apps

add app	▼

✖ Gmail - Email by Google   Universal iOS   Free
✖ TunnelBear VPN & Wifi ...   Universal iOS   Free

Figure 5-10. *The Add App button appears on the left side of the webpage with the two apps to be updated listed below it*

5. Repeat step 4 until you add the number of apps you want to update.

6. In the Devices section, click or tap Add Device Group and then select the group of iPhones that will receive the app updates in the Add Device Group drop-down list.

    The device group appears underneath the Add Device Group box.

7. If you only want to apply the update to a single iPhone, click or tap Add Device and then select the device that will receive the update in the Add Device drop-down list.

    The device appears underneath the Add Device box.

8. To the right of the Devices section, click or tap the
Update Apps button shown in Figure 5-11.

Figure 5-11. *The Update Apps button appears in the middle of the
button row below the Add App Group button*

In a short while, SimpleMDM pushes the update to all employee
iPhones that are scheduled to receive it. During the upgrade process, some
employees may notice that the affected app icons have the update timer
within the icon, which means the app is currently being updated and can't
be used until the update is complete.

CHAPTER 6

Recovering from Loss or Attack

Despite the best efforts by you and your employees to secure your iPhones, it's inevitable that an employee's iPhone will come under attack or an employee will lose their iPhone. For example, a phisher may successfully trick an employee into giving access to his iPhone. Or, your employee's iPhone may be lost in an accident, personal robbery, or as part of a theft of another item such as a car.

If your employees have taken well to your training, then the affected employee will report the theft or attack to you as soon as he possibly can. Once you're up to speed, it's time for you and your IT department to follow your company policy to lock the iPhone and then work to find and recover the iPhone if possible.

Although you can use an MDM system to find the iPhone, such as the Enable Lost Mode option in SimpleMDM, that system only sends a message to the reader to bring the iPhone back. The MDM system doesn't tell you where the iPhone is. You need to enable Apple's Find My iPhone service so your MDM system or the Find My iPhone app on another iPhone can get the approximate location of your lost iPhone.

If you have the employee's recovered or replacement iPhone and you need to restore data and settings from her last backup on iTunes, what happens if iTunes can't recognize the iPhone? Apple allows you to access two different iPhone recovery modes, Recovery Mode and DFU Mode, by requiring you to press iPhone buttons in a certain order depending on the iPhone you use. If neither of those modes result in iTunes recognizing the iPhone, then you need to contact Apple Support for guidance.

Using Find My iPhone

Apple pre-installs the Find My iPhone app on its iPhones (and iPads) so you can find the approximate location of a lost or stolen iPhone on another iPhone or an iPad. However, Find My iPhone functionality isn't turned on automatically. As part of setting up a new company iPhone for an employee, you (or an IT staffer) must activate Find My iPhone in the Settings screen.

Employees will see the Find My iPhone app on their Home screen as the app can't be deleted, but they won't be able to log into the Find My iPhone app without knowing the Apple ID used to log into the company iCloud account.

Adding iCloud

When your company doesn't have an iCloud account but has an Apple ID to log into other Apple services, or has no Apple ID at all, then you need to create a new Apple ID on the iCloud website (`https://www.icloud.com/`) by clicking the "Create yours now" text link under the Keep Me Signed In check box.

After you create your new Apple ID, verify that you have an iCloud account by entering your Apple ID and password on the iCloud website. After you log in, you can log back out and give authorized employees (such as IT department staff) this new Apple ID to log into the Find My iPhone app on their iPhones.

Restricting iCloud Access

If your company already has an iCloud account that any employee can access, then any employee who logs into the iCloud website on a PC or Mac web browser can use Find My iPhone on the website to see the locations of all employee iPhones. Though Find My iPhone on the website is password-protected, the username and password are the same ones used to log into the iCloud website. So a dishonest employee will know where nearby employee iPhones are and may try to steal one or more.

This security threat should convince your managers to move all data stored on iCloud to a different file sharing system and restrict the iCloud account to approved personnel. When the new file-sharing system is up and running, delete the iCloud account and Apple ID. Finally, create a new Apple ID and iCloud account and give the Apple ID information to those who need to know. You may also want to research website blockers for browsers on your computers to dissuade any employees from trying to access your new iCloud account.

Activate Find My iPhone

If one or more employees are already using their company or personal iPhones and need to activate Find My iPhone, give them these instructions:

1. Tap Settings in the Home screen.

2. Tap your name at the top of the Settings screen.

3. In the Settings screen, tap iCloud.

4. Swipe up in the iCloud screen until you see Find My iPhone.

5. Tap Find My iPhone.

6. In the Find My iPhone screen shown in Figure 6-1, swipe the Find My iPhone slider button to the right.

    The Find My iPhone service is now active and the iPhone location is being tracked.

7. Swipe the Send Last Location slider button from left to right so the iPhone will send its location to Apple when its battery is critically low—that is, when the iPhone is about to turn off for lack of power.

    After the iPhone sends its location to Apple, Find My iPhone will be able to find the iPhone within 24 hours after the battery shuts down.

Figure 6-1. *When you turn Find My iPhone on, the iPhone can't be erased and reactivated until you enter your Apple ID password*

Launch Find My iPhone

Now that Find My iPhone is activated, here's how you and members of your IT staff launch and set up the app on the iPhone:

1. Tap Find My iPhone on the Home page.

2. In the Find My iPhone screen, type the email address and password for the iCloud account in the appropriate boxes.

3. Tap Sign In.

4. Turn on Send Last Location by tapping Turn On in the window.

Now the Find My iPhone app searches for and lists all your Apple devices that have Find My iPhone turned on including iPhone(s), iPad(s) and Mac(s). If the iPhone is currently turned on, the dot next to the iPhone name is green, and a green mile button to the right of the iPhone name tells you approximately how many miles the iPhone is from your current location. A gray button means the iPhone isn't on or it's not connected to a network. And if the button is blue, that means the iPhone is the one you're currently using.

Under the map in the top half of the Find My iPhone screen (see Figure 6-2), swipe up and down in the list (if necessary) and then tap the iPhone name to view the approximate location of the phone in the full-screen map.

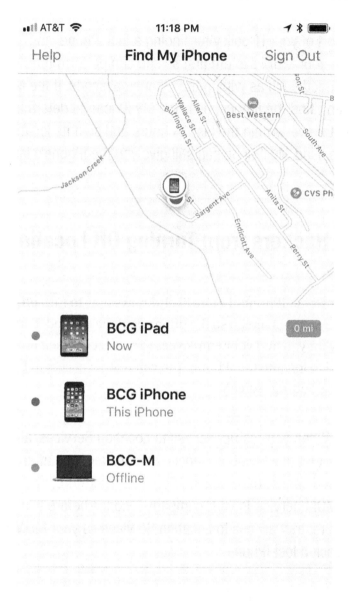

Figure 6-2. *A picture of the iPhone or iPad you're looking for appears within the map in the top half of the screen*

Tip   As part of your IT policy for finding a lost iPhone, an IT staffer should use your MDM system first so she can perform time-sensitive tasks if needed such as wiping the iPhone passcode. If the MDM system can't find the iPhone, use Find My iPhone to determine if the iPhone lost power within the last 24 hours and sent its location to Apple. If so, Find My iPhone can still give you the iPhone's last known location.

Restrict Hackers from Turning Off Location Services

A thief who's stolen iPhones before likely knows how to turn off Find My iPhone in the Settings screen so the phone can't be tracked. Fortunately, there's a way for you and your employees to protect yourself even if a thief has managed to log into the iPhone: You can restrict access to Location Services in the Settings screen.

Caution   When you restrict access to Location Services, all settings for all apps that use Location Services are locked, and afterward new apps you add cannot use Location Services. Therefore, you need to add your MDM service to your company iPhones before you or your employees restrict access to Location Services so your MDM service can still track a lost iPhone.

Here are the instructions to restrict Location Services on an iPhone that you can pass along to your employees after they've set up Find My iPhone:

1. Tap Settings in the Home screen.

2. Swipe up in the Settings screen until you see General.

3. Tap General.

4. Swipe up in the General screen until you see Restrictions.

5. Tap Restrictions.

6. In the Restrictions screen, tap Enable Restrictions.

7. In the Set Passcode screen, type a four-digit PIN that is different from the one you use to log into your iPhone.

8. Confirm your restrictions PIN by typing it again.

9. In the Restrictions screen, swipe up until you see Location Services.

10. Tap Location Services as shown in Figure 6-3.

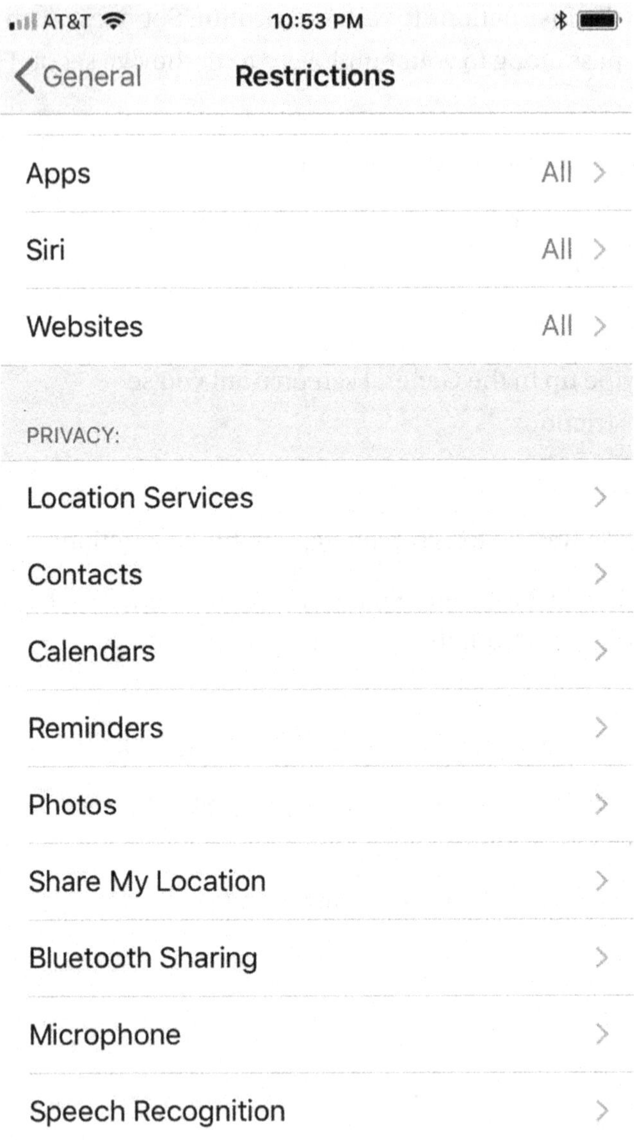

.ıll AT&T 🌣	10:53 PM	⚹ ▬▬

‹ General   **Restrictions**

Apps	All ›
Siri	All ›
Websites	All ›

PRIVACY:

Location Services	›
Contacts	›
Calendars	›
Reminders	›
Photos	›
Share My Location	›
Bluetooth Sharing	›
Microphone	›
Speech Recognition	›

Figure 6-3. *The Location Services option appears at the top of the Privacy section*

Note   If your iPhone goes into Sleep mode while you're in the Restrictions or Location Services screen, your screen will awaken in the General screen, where you must tap Restrictions and then enter your restrictions passcode to regain access to the Restrictions screen.

11.   In the Location Services screen, tap Don't Allow Changes.

12.   Tap Restrictions in the upper-left corner of the Location Services screen.

13.   Enable your restrictions by tapping General in the upper-left corner of the Restrictions screen.

The next time you tap Restrictions in the General screen, you'll have to enter your restrictions PIN.

It's recommended not to set this up before you give the employee the iPhone so the iPhone user can set and remember her own PIN for changing restrictions. You should also recommend that the employee change her restrictions PIN (and her iPhone PIN) often.

Take Actions

If you need to get driving instructions to find the iPhone (either for company security personnel charged with finding the iPhone and/or the police), or if you need to lock the iPhone, tap Actions at the bottom center of the screen.

At the bottom of the Actions screen below the map, use one of the following buttons:

- Tap the car icon to the right of the iPhone name to open the Maps app and view a full-screen map with driving directions to the approximate location of the iPhone. Return to the Actions screen within the Find My iPhone app by tapping Find iPhone in the upper-left corner of the screen.

- If you think the iPhone may be nearby, tap Play Sound to have your lost iPhone play a loud pinging sound. If you can hear it, follow the pinging sound until you find the iPhone.

- Turn on Lost Mode to lock and track your missing iPhone by tapping Lost Mode and then tapping the Turn On Lost Mode button. Then you can add a phone number where you can be reached and a message for the person reading the note.

- Erase the remote iPhone by tapping Erase iPhone and then tapping the Erase iPhone button.

Note   If you're managing Lost Mode or the erasure of the iPhone data from SimpleMDM or another MDM system, you don't need to use Lost Mode or Erase iPhone within Find My iPhone.

When you're done, tap All in the upper-left corner of the Actions screen to return to the Find My iPhone screen.

Using Recovery Mode

When you connect a recovered or replacement iPhone to iTunes on your computer to restore the apps and data from a previous iTunes backup, iTunes may say it doesn't recognize the iPhone and/or you may see one of the following displays or messages on the iPhone screen:

- Your screen displays the Apple logo for several minutes and does not show a progress bar.

- The progress bar on the iPhone screen does nothing for several minutes.

- You see the Connect to iTunes message screen instead of the Lock screen.

In these cases, the solution may be as simple as replacing the iPhone cable with a new one and reconnecting your iPhone and computer. If that doesn't work, Apple gives you two methods to try to recover the iPhone so you can back up your data: Recovery Mode or DFU (Device Firmware Update) Mode. You need to connect the iPhone to your computer that has iTunes running so iTunes can attempt to recover your iPhone with either Recovery Mode or DFU Mode.

If your employee backed up her iPhone with iTunes, then once you've recovered, she can to plug her iPhone into your computer, access her iTunes account, and recover her last backup that includes apps, settings, and data. If her data is saved elsewhere, then you'll need to reinstall the appropriate app on her iPhone to restore that data as well as push all the apps and settings from your MDM system to that iPhone before she can start restoring her data.

Caution   If the iPhone is not backed up, then all data and settings on the iPhone are deleted during the restoration process and the iPhone is returned to its original settings.

It's likely that your company has one of the most recent iPhone models available: the iPhone 8, the iPhone 8 Plus, or the iPhone X, which were all introduced in 2017. However, if you let your employees use their own devices, they may have the older iPhone 6s, 6s Plus, 7, or 7 Plus. Because Apple is still selling these older iPhones as of this writing (late Spring 2018), this chapter also covers how to access Recovery Mode in iPhone 6s-series and 7-series iPhones.

The instructions in this section presume that the buttons on the iPhone are working properly. If they're not, then you'll need to contact Apple Support as you'll learn about later in this chapter.

iPhone 8, iPhone 8 Plus, and iPhone X

Although the iPhone 8 and 8 Plus have Home buttons, the iPhone X does not. Therefore, Apple decided to use the same method for accessing Recovery Mode for all three of its 2017-model iPhones. Here's how to activate Recovery Mode:

1.   Close iTunes on your computer if it's open.

2.   Turn off the iPhone if it isn't off already.

3.   Connect the iPhone cable to a USB port on your computer.

4.   Press and quickly release the Volume Up button.

5.   Press and quickly release the Volume Down button.

6. Press and hold the Power button (also known as the Sleep/Wake button) even after you see the Apple logo on the screen.

7. Release the button when you see the Connect to iTunes screen.

8. Open iTunes on your computer.

On your computer screen, you should see a pop-up window that says, "There is a problem with the iPhone that requires it to be updated or restored." Click Restore to restore the iPhone (see Figure 6-4).

Figure 6-4. If Find My iPhone is enabled, you need to enter your Apple ID password before you can restore the iPhone

After you click Restore, iTunes will automatically restore your most recent backup if it detects that you used it to back up to iCloud or your computer.

If you decide you don't need to restore the iPhone, click Cancel in the pop-up window, and then restart the iPhone by pressing the Power button until the Contact to iTunes screen disappears. Then press and hold the Power button until the Apple logo appears on the screen.

iPhone 7 and 7 Plus

Follow these steps to activate Recovery Mode on the iPhone 7 or 7 Plus:

1. Turn off iTunes on your computer if it's on already.

2. Connect the iPhone 7 or 7 Plus cable to a USB port on your computer.

3. Press and hold down the Power button (also known as the Sleep/Wake button) and the Volume Down button until the screen turns off.

4. Continue holding the Power and Volume Down buttons even after you see the Apple logo on the screen.

5. Release the buttons when you see the Connect to iTunes message on the screen.

6. Launch iTunes on your computer.

Within iTunes, you see a message that states, "There is a problem with the iPhone that requires it to be updated or restored." Click Restore. If you backed up your iPhone to iCloud or your computer, then the iPhone will restore your iPhone from that backup copy.

Abort the restoration process by pressing and holding the Power and Volume down button at the same time until the Apple logo appears on the screen.

iPhone 6s and 6s Plus

Here's how to enable Recovery Mode on the iPhone 6s and 6s Plus:

1. Turn off the iPhone if it isn't off already.

2. Press and hold down the Home button on the iPhone.

3. Plug the iPhone 6s or 6s Plus into your computer USB port.

4. Release the Home button when the Connect to iTunes message appears on the screen.

iTunes opens and a pop-up window appears on the screen asking you to either update or restore the iPhone. Click Restore to restore the iPhone and the most recent backed up data you saved to iCloud or your computer. If you did not back up the iPhone to iCloud or your computer, then all data and settings on the iPhone will be deleted.

Restoring the iPhone from DFU Mode

If Recovery Mode doesn't work, then your last chance to restore the iPhone is to place it in Device Firmware Upgrade (DFU) Mode. DFU Mode can also get the iPhone back in contact with iTunes so you can try to restore the iPhone.

As with Recovery Mode, there are different instructions for entering DFU Mode on the latest iPhone 8, 8 Plus, and iPhone X compared with the older iPhone 7 and 6s models. These instructions require you to pay more attention to how long you press and hold buttons on the iPhone.

As with placing the iPhone into Recovery Mode, these instructions presume that all the buttons on your iPhone are working properly. If they're not, it's time to contact Apple Support as you'll learn about later in this chapter.

iPhone 8 and X Models

If you're using the iPhone 8, 8 Plus, or iPhone X, here's how to access DFU Mode:

1. Plug the iPhone cable into a USB port on your computer.

2. Launch iTunes if it isn't open already.

3. Turn off the iPhone if it's not off already.

4. Press and hold on the Power button for 3 seconds.

5. Press and hold down the Volume Down button while you continue to hold down the Power button.

6. Hold both buttons down for 10 seconds.

   If you see the Apple logo, you'll have to restart and go back to Step 3.

7. Release the Power button but keeping holding the Volume Down button for 5 seconds.

If the screen stays black, that means you are in DFU Mode and iTunes should recognize the iPhone and ask if you want to restore it as described earlier in this chapter. If iTunes still doesn't recognize your iPhone, contact Apple Support as you'll learn about later in this chapter.

When you need to get out of DFU Mode, here's how to return your iPhone to normal operation:

1. Press and release the Volume Up button.

2. Press and release the Volume Down button.

3. Press and hold the Power button until you see the Apple logo on the screen.

iPhone 7 Models

Follow these instructions to enter DFU Mode on the iPhone 7 or 7 Plus:

1. Plug the iPhone into a USB port on your computer.

2. Launch iTunes if it isn't open already.

3. Turn the iPhone off if it isn't already.

4. Press and hold the Power and Volume Down buttons on the iPhone simultaneously for 10 seconds.

5. Release the Power button and keep holding the Volume Down button for another 10 seconds.

iTunes should recognize the iPhone and ask you if you want to update or restore it as discussed earlier in this chapter. If iTunes doesn't recognize the iPhone, contact Apple Support as you'll learn about later in this chapter.

When you want to exit DFU Mode, press and hold the Power and Volume Down buttons simultaneously until the Apple logo appears on the screen.

iPhone 6 Models

Here's how to turn on DFU mode on your iPhone 6 or 6S:

1. Connect your iPhone cable to a USB port on your computer.

2. Launch iTunes if it's not already running.

3. Turn off your iPhone if it's not off already.

4. Press and hold the Power button at the top of the iPhone for 3 seconds.

5. Press and hold the Home button as you continue to hold the Power button.

6. Continue to hold the Home and Power buttons simultaneously for 10 seconds.

    If you see the Apple logo on the screen, then you'll need to restart the process starting at step 3.

7. Release the Power button but continue to hold the Home button for 5 seconds.

    If you see the Plug into iTunes screen, then you'll have to start over beginning with step 3.

8. Release the Home button.

If the screen is black, then you are in DFU mode. iTunes should recognize your iPhone and ask you if you want to update or restore your iPhone as you learned about earlier in this chapter. You can return to normal mode by pressing the Power button until you see the Apple logo on the screen.

If Nothing's Working

If you still can't restore the iPhone using Recovery Mode or DFU Mode, or if you have damaged buttons on the iPhone that prevent you from entering either of these modes, then you can access the Apple iPhone Support page at https://support.apple.com/iphone (see Figure 6-5). Tap Contact Support in the upper-right corner of the webpage to contact an Apple Support representative directly.

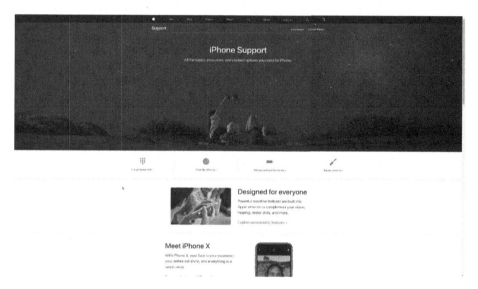

Figure 6-5. *The Contact Support option appears underneath the black menu bar*

Index

Printed in the United States
By Bookmasters